MULTIMODAL PSYCHIATRIC MUSIC THERAPY

FOR
ADULTS
ADOLESCENTS
AND CHILDREN

A CLINICAL MANUAL

Michael D. Cassity, Ph.D., RMT-BC

Julia E. Cassity, M.S., RMT-BC

MMB

MMB MUSIC, INC.

MULTIMODAL PSYCHIATRIC MUSIC THERAPY FOR ADULTS, ADOLESCENTS AND CHILDREN
A Clinical Manual

Second Edition
Michael D. Cassity, Ph.D., RMT-BC
Julia E. Cassity, M.S., RMT-BC

First printing: October, 1995
Printed in USA
ISBN: 0-918812-85-2

For further information and catalogs, contact:

MMB Music, Inc.
Contemporary Arts Building
3526 Washington Avenue
Saint Louis, MO 63103-1019

Phone: 314 531-9635, 800 543-3771 (USA/Canada)
Fax: 314 531-8384

CONTENTS

I. ADULTS

Page

BEHAVIOR

B-1   Lack of assertiveness 1
B-2   Lack of attention span...2
B-3   Lack of awareness of personal space/boundaries 3
B-4   Poor eye contact..3
B-5   Demanding and intrusive (overly assertive)...4
B-6   Passive dependent or passive aggressive communication 4
B-7   Lacks self-control; loses temper 4
B-8   Assaultive behavior..5
B-9   Inappropriate channeling of creativity 5
B-10   Rocks while seated 5
B-11   Excessive complaining 5
B-12   Exhibits general perseverative behaviors..5
B-13   Restlessness; akathisia 5
B-14   Intolerance of younger age groups of patients...5

AFFECT

A-1   Inability to verbally or nonverbally express or identify feelings
       or emotions in self or others; flat or inappropriate affect.................................6
A-2   Exhibits emotional detachment regarding life situations 9
A-3   Becomes angry when coping with frustration 9
A-4   Exhibits hyperactive or manic behavior...10
A-5   Depressive; decreased energy; pessimistic about future.................................10
A-6   Severe depression; suicidal ideation..11
A-7   Anxiety...12
A-8   Impulsive emotional outbursts; lacks impulse control 12
A-9   Panic attack 12
A-10   Angry, emotional outbursts; intermittent explosive disorder 13
A-11   Feels "out of control" when listening to certain songs...................................13
A-12   Difficulty identifying perceived unacceptable or suppressed feelings 13
A-13   Experience anger when attention is given to other clients 14
A-14   Expresses affect inappropriate to a particular emotion 14
A-15   Intellectualizes feelings...14
A-16   Inability or unwillingness to empathize with others.......................................14
A-17   Alternates between manic and depressive episodes; bipolar 14
A-18   Difficulty relating to staff that is the same sex as the abuser 14
A-19   Feelings of rage and resentment toward mother 15

SENSORY

S-1   Preoccupation with internal thoughts; hallucinations 15
S-2   Difficulty coping with stress and tension..16

IMAGERY

IM-1   Difficulty envisioning a pleasant place during relaxation 16
IM-2   Difficulty focusing on pleasant place for 10 to 15 minutes 16
IM-3   Distorted body image (associated with eating disorder)...17

COGNITIVE

C-1   Low self esteem; low opinion of self; negative self statements 17
C-2   Delusional; paranoid ideation; does not trust peers 18
C-3   Lacks problem solving skills...19
C-4   Disoriented; lacks reality orientation; loose associations...21
C-5   Poor short/long term memory skills 21
C-6   Poor decision-making skills 22
C-7   Denies having problems 22
C-8   Does not accept responsibility for change 23
C-9   Gives up easily when solving problems 23
C-10   Difficulty following directions 23
C-11   Unaware of the purpose or need for hospitalization 24
C-12   Difficulty coping with the reality of hopitalization 24
C-13   Denies others have similar problems 24
C-14   Has difficulties in verbal psychotherapy 24
C-15   Delusions of grandeur..25
C-16   Poor judgement; difficulty assessing social situations...25
C-17   Lack of self-awareness 25
C-18   Difficulty setting goals...25
C-19   Misinterprets messages/communications 25
C-20   Feelings of helplessness 26
C-21   Inability to structure time..26
C-22   Inability to relate to metaphor 26
C-23   Lacks concept of a healthy heterosexual relationship..26

INTERPERSONAL – SOCIALIZATION (Includes Leisure Skills)

IS-1   Reclusive; withdrawn; isolative behavior..26
IS-2   Does not appropriately utilize leisure time 30
IS-3   Uncooperative behavior with others...31
IS-4   Lack of interest and motivation to use leisure time 32
IS-5   Experiences difficulty bonding with others 33
IS-6   Experiences difficulty with the sharing of personal data...34
IS-7   Difficulty involving self in community groups 34
IS-8   Does not sit with group 35
IS-9   Inappropriate relationships with opposite sex..35
IS-10   Self centeredness 35
IS-11   Undesirable statements about others; "loner" 36
IS-12   Wears clothing inappropriate for the occasion 36
IS-13   Egocentric, childish behavior 36
IS-14   Inappropriate verbalization in social setting 36
IS-15   Attention seeking 37
IS-16   Poor group leadership and organizational skills 37
IS-17   Frequents barrooms during leisure time 37
IS-18   Demonstrates lack of awareness of others...37
IS-19   Difficulty learning names of long term relationships 37
IS-20   Difficulty tolerating small groups..37
IS-21   Inappropriate relationships with the opposite sex 38

IS-22   Aggressive and manipulative..38
IS-23   Lacks knowledge of how to have nondestructive fun..38
IS-24   Exhibits inappropriate behavior at community events 38
IS-25   Argues frequently with authority figures...38
IS-26   Interacts with staff but not with peers...38
IS-27   Impatience and intolerance with peers 38
IS-28   Excessive working; lack of leisure 39
IS-29   Excessive stress associated with leisure activity 39
IS-30   Withdrawn and passive during one-to-one sessions 39
IS-31   Stays in bed all day; avoids socialization 39
IS-32   Will not attend group 39

DRUGS (includes D-1.0 Substance Use or Abuse and Medications; D-2.0 Physical Well Being; D-3.0 Physical Communication Problems)

D-1.1   Abuses substances during leisure time 40
D-1.2   Denies having a substance abuse problem 40
D-1.3   Attributes substance abuse to life stress..41
D-1.4   Lacks awareness of the progression of substance abuse 41
D-1.5   Reluctant to discuss substance abuse and treatment issues...............................41
D-1.6   Manipulates environment to get own way 42
D-1.7   Inability to identify coping mechanisms 42
D-1.8   Mourns loss of drug habit 42

D-2.1   Absence of daily exercise routine; poor muscle tone 42
D-2.2   Poor personal hygiene 42
D-2.3   Insomnia 42
D-2.4   Lack of neuromuscular endurance in upper extremities 42
D-2.5   Poor gross and fine motor coordination 43
D-2.6   Sensory integrative functioning 43
D-2.7   Sensorimotor functioning...43
D-2.8   Lack of diaphragmatic control 44

D-3.1   Does not communicate clearly; poor articulation...44
D-3.2   Poor nonverbal communication 45
D-3.3   Uses one-word sentences...45
D-3.4   Exhibits pressured speech 45
D-3.5   Makes irrelevant comments about topic of group discussion 45
D-3.6   Poor breath support...45
D-3.7   Speaks too softly to be heard 45

Code 46

II. ADOLESCENTS

BEHAVIOR
B-1 · Lack of assertiveness...47
B-2 · Attention deficit disorder..47
B-3 Withdrawal...48
B-4 Hyperactive; unable to focus..48
B-5 Inability to follow directions...48

AFFECT
A-1 · Inability to identify/express feelings; inappropriate expression of feelings......................48
A-2 Exhibits anger or rage...49
A-3 Experiences stress reactions...51
A-4 Experiences excessive anxiety..51
A-5 Lacks self control; poor impulse control..52
A-6 Difficulty sharing feelings..52
A-7 Depressed...52
A-8 Suicidal..53
A-9 Difficulty expressing positive feelings...53
A-10 Socially unacceptable expression of emotions..53

SENSORY 53

IMAGERY
IM-1 Distorted body image (associated with eating disorder)...53

COGNITIVE
C-1 · Low self-esteem; negative self statements..54
C-2 Lacks problem solving skills...54
C-3 Gives up easily when solving problems; low frustration tolerance...................................56
C-4 Exhibits paranoid behavior...56
C-5 Does not respond well to constructive criticism...56
C-6 Lacks awareness of personal problems...57
C-7 Poor organizational skills...57
C-8 Poor conflict identification and resolution skills...57
C-9 Inability to cope with family conflicts..57
C-10 Lacks insight into family interactions..58
C-11 Unaware of relationship to peer group...58
C-12 Does not trust therapist..58
C-13 Inability to make decisions...58

INTERPERSONAL-SOCIALIZATION (includes Leisure Skills)
IS-1 Uncooperative behavior; does not follow directions..58
IS-2 Lacks awareness of self or others; detached...60
IS-3 Withdrawn; isolates self...61
IS-4 Inappropriate use of leisure time...62
IS-5 Lacks motivation to engage in leisure activities..63
IS-6 Lack of interest in others..63
IS-7 Excessive fear of rejection...63
IS-8 Uses inappropriate behavior to gain attention...63
IS-9 Does not share or take turns..64
IS-10 Poor leadership skills...64

DRUGS (includes D-1.0 Substance Use Or Abuse)
D-1.1 Unaware of or denies substance abuse 64
D-1.2 Uses substances regularly 65
D-1.3 Uses substances to numb affect 65
D-1.4 Mourns loss of the substance 65
D-1.5 Links own identity to substance 65
D-1.6 Lack of diaphragmatic control (from eating disorder) 65

Code 66

III. CHILDREN

BEHAVIOR
B-1 Unassertive; does not express own needs 67
B-2 Attention deficit; lacks attention span 68
B-3 Does not take turns 68
B-4 Hits peers 68
B-5 Poor eye contact 69

AFFECT
A-1 Impaired ability to identify/express feelings;
     Inappropriate affect; poor vocabulary of feeling words 69

SENSORY
S-1 Lacks auditory sequential memory 70
S-2 Lacks auditory discrimination skills 71

IMAGERY
IM-1 Inability to experience thoughts when attempting to relax 71
IM-2 Inability to use imagination to develop stories 71

COGNITIVE
C-1 Difficulty following directions 72
C-2 Lacks directionality and spatial concepts 72
C-3 Low self-esteem; negative self-statements 73
C-4 Inappropriate approach to tasks 73
C-5 Manipulates using intimidation 73
C-6 Lacks temporal or time concepts 73
C-7 Lacks money concepts 74
C-8 Difficulty recalling letters of the alphabet 74
C-9 Poor counting skills 74
C-10 Poor reading and writing skills 74

INTERPERSONAL-SOCIALIZATION
IS-1 Exhibits disruptive or socially inappropriate behavior 74
IS-2 Withdrawal 75
IS-3 Uncooperative with adults and peers 76

IS-4   Does not share 77
IS-5   Interrupts 77
IS-6   Inaudible speaking voice 78
IS-7   Lacks leadership skills 78
IS-8   Does not respond to greetings or closings 78

DRUGS (includes D-1.0 Physical Well Being and D-2.0 Physical Communication Problems)

D-1.1   Impaired gross motor coordination 78
D-1.2   Lacks finger dexterity 79
D-1.3   Impaired grasp function 79
D-1.4   Lacks eye-hand motor coordination 79
D-1.5   Excessive dropping of objects (poor grasp maintenance) 79

D-2.1   Impaired ability to describe objects, feelings or situations 80
D-2.2   Difficulty imitating speech or nonspeech sounds 80
D-2.3   Explosive speech 80
D-2.4   Poor speech articulation 80
D-2.5   Impaired receptive language ability; poor comprehension 80

Code 80

IV. ADULTS: MUSIC BEHAVIOR

LISTENING TO MUSIC

L-1   Demonstrates musical preferences 82
L-2   Demonstrates familiarity with a variety of styles of music 84
L-3   Shares personal knowledge or recollections of music 84
L-4   Chooses music to promote own relaxation 85
L-5   Selects preferred music that expresses feelings 85
L-6   Demonstrates musical awareness 86
L-7   Associates affect with corresponding music 86
L-8   Recognizes titles of songs when they are played 87
L-9   Chooses a song for group listening 87
L-10   Distinguishes characteristics of music 87
L-11   Listens to music but does not identify musical preferences 88
L-12   Chooses music that describes self 88
L-13   Identifies names of musical instruments used in a recording 88
L-14   Demonstrates the ability to perceive music 88
L-15   Sleeps when listening to music 88
L-16   Patient listens to one recording to exclusion of other recordings 89
L-17   Demonstrates knowledge of relaxing music 89
L-18   Uses musical equipment independently 89
L-19   Listens to music independently 89
L-20   Demonstrates the ability to locate sound sources 89
L-21   Chooses music that describes a peer 89
L-22   Prefers specific elements of music 89
L-23   Expresses likes as well as dislikes regarding music 89
L-24   Chooses appropriate background music 90

SINGING

S-1   Participates in group sing-a-long 90
S-2   Performs a vocal solo before the group 91
S-3   Sings and follows a choral part 91
S-4   Participates in a choir 92
S-5   Completes music questionnaire 92
S-6   Exhibits superior vocal skill 92
S-7   Sings only one style of music 93
S-8   Demonstrates vocal range 93
S-9   Sings at least two lines of a song from memory 93
S-10   Sings with correct pitch and rhythm 93
S-11   Matches pitch 93
S-12   Sings with appropriate dynamics 94
S-13   Requests voice lessons 94
S-14   Uses voice expressively 94
S-15   Stays on task during singing activities 94
S-16   Sings with breath control and appropriate intensity 94
S-17   Participates in toning exercises 94
S-18   Sings both acappella and with accompaniment 95
S-19   Demonstrates physiological aspects of vocalization 95
S-20   Sings lyrics to an entire song 95
S-21   Sings lyrics to only phrases of songs 95
S-22   Sings song lyrics in sequence 95
S-23   Exhibits performance anxiety 95
S-24   Expresses likes and dislikes about a song 95

PLAYING INSTRUMENTS

P-1   Demonstrates interest in playing music instrument 96
P-2   Demonstrates instrumental ability 97
P-3   Exhibits performance anxiety 97
P-4   Performs in a group ensemble for peers 98
P-5   Assessment of past instrumental performance 98
P-6   Imitates of repeats rhythmic or melodic phrase 98
P-7   Accompanies own singing 99
P-8   Plays tone bells 99
P-9   Participates in informal "jam session" 99
P-10   Performs a variety of musical styles 99

IMPROVISING MUSIC

I-1   Plays Orff and rhythm instruments 99
I-2   Expresses feelings and expressiveness 100
I-3   Maintains ostinato pattern 101
I-4   Improvises a rhythm or melody over an ostinato pattern 101
I-5   Feels musically inferior 101
I-6   Demonstrates preference for improvisational instruments 102
I-7   Demonstrates the ability to imitate, alternate, and initiate 102
I-8   Expresses a desire to improvise at the piano 102
I-9   Expresses creativity during group improvisation 102
I-10   Feels at ease when improvising 103
I-11   Leads or conducts group improvisation sessions 103
I-12   "Hears" chord changes 103

I-13   Interacts with other group members while improvising 103
I-14   Improvises movements to music 103

LOCOMOTOR MOVEMENT TO MUSIC
LM-1   Dances to music 104
LM-2   Participates in structured creative movement to music 104
LM-3   Participates in unstructured creative movement to music 104
LM-4   Moves in rhythm to music 105
LM-5   Participates in aerobics 105
LM-6   Maintains the tempo of the music given directed movement 105
LM-7   Integrates and performs structured rhythm patterns to music 105
LM-8   Participates in creative dance and body language 106
LM-9   Awareness of personal space or body limits 106
LM-10 Leads group in movement 106
LM-11 Feels comfortable with structured movement activity 106

COMPOSING MUSIC
C-1   Participates in lyric writing 106
C-2   Composes, sings, and plays own compositions 107
C-3   Learns newly composed song by rote 107

NONLOCOMOTOR MOVEMENT TO MUSIC
NL-1   Imitates movements to music 108
NL-2   Changes movement in response to music 108
NL-3   Taps fingers, toes, or claps to music 108
NL-4   Follows and maintains pulse 108

Code 108

V. ADOLESCENTS: MUSIC BEHAVIOR

LISTENING TO MUSIC
L-1   Demonstrates awareness of a variety of styles of music 110
L-2   Demonstrates musical preferences 111
L-3   Uses music for relaxation 112
L-4   Associates affect with music 112
L-5   Interested in new types of music 112
L-6   Chooses music that expresses own views 112
L-7   Identifies musical characteristics 112
L-8   Has confidence in own musical interpretations 112
L-9   Listens to the lyrics of music 112
L-10   Attends to music 113

PLAYING INSTRUMENTS
P-1   Desires to play an instrument 113
P-2   Plays instrument for others 114
P-3   Participates in group ensemble 114
P-4   Critiques musical performance 114

P-5 Demonstrates rhythmic ability...115
P-6 Respects various musical styles 115

IMPROVISING MUSIC

I-1 Varies improvisation...115
I-2 Improvises within rhythmic structure 116
I-3 Demonstrates awareness of other ensemble members......................................116
I-4 Demonstrates interest in playing music instruments 116
I-5 Improvises on the pentatonic scale 116
I-6 Improvises on the blues scale...116
I-7 Creates improvisations representative of moods..116
I-8 Improvises with one other person 116
I-9 Improvises musically..117

SINGING

S-1 Demonstrates the ability to match pitch and follow rhythms 117
S-2 Sings solo in front of group..117
S-3 Blends with group 117
S-4 Sings with adequate loudness..118
S-5 Sings with a vocal tone that is not too breathy...118
S-6 Sings in tune with a pleasing timbre...118
S-7 Sings with proper diction 118
S-8 Demonstrates expanded vocal range...118
S-9 Sings with a choir..119

COMPOSING MUSIC

C-1 Demonstrates the ability to write lyrics and melody...119
C-2 Uses lyric writing as a means of self expressions...119
C-3 Participates in writing song parodies..119
C-4 Bases music composition on pictures, themes, or symbols 119
C-5 Experiences rhythmic difficulties when composing 120
C-6 Composes a variety of styles of music...120
C-7 Has trouble rhyming or thinking of lyrics 120
C-8 Uses imagination to create music productions..120
C-9 Organizes sounds into music 120

LOCOMOTOR MOVEMENT TO MUSIC

LM-1 Participates in unstructured creative movement to music 120
LM-2 Dances to music 121
LM-3 Unable to respond to cues when dancing...121

Code 121

VI. CHILDHOOD: MUSIC BEHAVIOR

LISTENING TO MUSIC
L-1	Identifies characteristics of music	122
L-2	States musical preferences	123
L-3	Reads lyrics to songs	123
L-4	Identifies popular songs	123
L-5	Demonstrates audience behavior	123

SINGING
S-1	Sings on pitch	123
S-2	Sings melodic phrases	124
S-3	Sings with music therapist from song book	124
S-4	Sing entire length of song	124
S-5	Sing loudly enough to be heard	124
S-6	Chooses songs about own family from song books	124
S-7	Sings a song from memory	125

PLAYING INSTRUMENTS
P-1	Responds rhythmically to music	125
P-2	Plays a variety of instruments	125
P-3	Plays instrument on cue	125
P-4	Plays autoharp	125
P-5	Plays choir chimes	126
P-6	Plays guitar	126
P-7	Uses rhythm or lumi sticks correctly	126
P-8	Listens to tape recording of own performance	126
P-9	Plays music instrument for peer or staff	126

LOCOMOTOR MOVEMENT TO MUSIC
LM-1	Creates movement to music	126
LM-2	Participates in choreography	127
LM-3	Imitates or mirrors musical movement	127
LM-4	Moves in rhythm to music	127
LM-5	Moves freely and spontaneously without rigidity	127
LM-6	Follows sequence of movement activity	127
LM-7	Walks to the beat of the music	127

COMPOSING MUSIC
C-1	Composes new lyrics to songs	128
C-2	Composes a greeting song	128

IMPROVISING MUSIC
I-1	Creates song through improvisation	128
I-2	Directs an improvisation	129

NONLOCOMOTOR MOVEMENT TO MUSIC
NL-1	Claps rhythms	129

Code	129

Appendix I: About This Manual 130
    Origin of Data 130
    Evolution of the Model 132
    Description of the Model 135
    Most Frequent Modalities in Psychiatric Music Therapy 141

Appendix II: Tutorial Guide: Use of This Manual 144
    Initial Assessment 145
    Program Planning 145
    Case Example: Adults 145
        Case of *D* 146
        Multimodal Music Therapy Profile 147
        Music Therapy Intervention Plan 151
        Implementation Strategy 152
    Case Examples: Adolescence 154
        Case of *M* 155
        Multimodal Music Therapy Profile 156
        Music Therapy Intervention Plan 158
        Implementation Strategy 159
        Case of *B* 161
        Multimodal Music Therapy Profile 163
    Case Example: Childhood 164
        Case of *J* 164
        Multimodal Music Therapy Profile 166
        Music Therapy Intervention Plan 169
        Implementation Strategy 170
    Practice Exercises 172
        Case Study I, Adults: Sickly 173
        Case Study II, Adults: Hungarian Opera Singer 180
        Case Study III, Childhood: No One Hits The Baby 187

Appendix III: *Psychiatric Music Therapy Questionnaire*: Adults 194

Appendix IV: *Psychiatric Music Therapy Questionnaire*: Adolescents 206

Appendix V: *Psychiatric Music Therapy Questionnaire*: Childhood 217

Appendix VI: Clinical Forms 228

References 236

ABOUT THE AUTHORS

Michael D. Cassity is Associate Professor and Director of Music Therapy at Southwestern Oklahoma State University. Michael has a B.A. degree in psychology from Southwest Baptist University, a Master of Music Therapy from Loyola University (New Orleans), and a Ph.D. with a major in music therapy from the University of Iowa.

Julia E. Cassity is a caseworker–music therapist and director of Bright Beginnings, the therapeutic nursery at New Horizons Community Mental Health Center, Weatherford, Oklahoma. She also is a member of the adjunct psychology faculty at Southwestern Oklahoma State University. Julia has a B.S. in music therapy from Texas Woman's University and a Master of Science in applied clinical psychology from Southwestern Oklahoma State University.

ACKNOWLEDGMENTS

The authors wish to express appreciation to the Oklahoma State Regents for Higher Education, Edward Daniel Dill, Ph.D., and Charles W. Chapman, Ph.D. for funding the initial research that made the writing of this book possible. Appreciation also is expressed to Jenifer Nail for clerical assistance, Gary Blodgett and Ann Kiser for their assistance in processing the data, and to the music therapy clinical training directors who furnished the initial data for this study. This manual is dedicated to Professor Emeritus Charles Braswell for his 36 years of service to the music therapy profession at Loyola University, New Orleans.

PSYCHIATRIC MUSIC THERAPY ASSESSMENTS AND TREATMENTS EMPLOYED IN NAMT-APPROVED CLINICAL TRAINING FACILITIES: ADULTS

(Combined, $N = 541$; Male, $N1 = 260$; 48.06% Female, $N2 = 281$; 51.94%)

ASSESSMENT AREA

BEHAVIOR (Combined, $n = 55$; 10.17%; Male, $n1 = 24$; 43.64%; Female, $n2 = 31$; 56.36%)

PROBLEM   MUSIC THERAPY INTERVENTION

B-1   Lack of assertiveness resulting in the inability to meet or communicate needs; passivity; difficulty verbalizing needs, feelings, likes and dislikes; does not express own views on a topic during a discussion ($n3 = 5$; $n4 = 9$; $n5 = 14$; 25.45%)

Give client experience at identifying assertive/nonassertive messages in song lyrics during music listening-discussion activity. M-30; F-30

Encourage controlled, honest verbalization of thoughts, feelings, and needs through the use of certain songs that appeal to the emotions. F-35

The clients each select a song to be played during the session. They then work with a partner to negotiate which of the two songs selected will be played for the group. Only one song may be played. M-41; F-41

*   *   *   *

The clients each select one song from song books for the group to sing, then tell why they selected the song. M-41; F-41

Have the group sing the song, "My Favorite Things." Each client will then list the things they enjoy the most and communicate them to the group. M-35;   F-32

*   *   *   *

Have the client write a song titled "Everybody's Bill of Rights." Let the client fill in key words. M-51; F-51

Write the lyrics of a familiar song on pieces of cardboard (one lyric written on each piece of cardboard). Seat the group in a circle and distribute the pieces of cardboard to the group members. Ask the group to work together by taking turns finding the words of the song title, or putting the lyrics in order. To achieve this task, each client must take turns communicating her need for a lyric that a person is holding. F-30

* * * *

Have the clients toss a ball to one another in the presence of background music. When the music stops, the person holding the ball will verbally respond to a question posed by the therapist. F-30

* * * *

During the music therapy discussion, call on specific clients, asking each client to verbalize at least one statement. F-35

B-2   Lack of attention span; does not remain on task long enough to express self; has difficulty concentrating (n3 = 4; n4 = 6; n5 = 10; 18.16%)

Involve client in structured improvisation over a chordal background. Allow client to play several instruments during a single session. M-40; F-50

Structure instrumental instruction to enhance on-task behavior and concentration (e.g., plays entire piano composition without stopping). M-51; F-51

Using an alphabet chart, have the patient rewrite (convert) their name into musical notes. The patient then plays their name on the xylophone followed by improvisation of how they feel or their present mood. F-39

Involve the patient in a hand bell choir in which the patient must ring her assigned bell when the conductor points to her letter on the hand bell chart. F-50

* * * *

Direct the client's attention to the musical task (e.g., singing selected song) with verbal reinforcement for completion of the task. M-32; F-39

* * * *

Involve the client in a "fill in the blank" song writing activity. M-40; F-50

B-3   Lacks awareness of personal space/boundaries; interrupts others during group discussion; displays inappropriate verbal/nonverbal social behavior toward peers; exhibits lack of boundaries with peers and staff
(n3 = 4; n4 = 3; n5 = 7; 12.73%)

Conduct one-to-one music therapy sessions with the client, utilizing activities such as improvisation and musical role playing. M-25

Place the resident in a structured music therapy group (e.g., a performing group such as a choir) and provide counseling about proper social skills in group situations; explain the structure and rules of the activity. M-25-30; F-31

* * * *

Utilize music and movement activities with an emphasis on space, touch, and boundaries. F-35

* * * *

Have a group song writing activity which focuses on personal relationships. F-60

* * * *

During music discussion group, redirect speaking to appropriate times.
M-32

B-4   Poor eye contact; difficulty initiating conversation (n3 = 3; n4 = 2; n5 = 5; 9.09%)

Pass a ball around the circle to background music. When the music stops, the client holding the ball must draw a question from the "hat," read the question, then ask his neighbor the question. M-30

Use a mirroring activity to music. Have the client select a partner and mirror the partner's movements to increase eye contact and level of comfort. F-60

* * * *

Involve client in an Orff instrumental activity which requires eye contact for the following of cues. M-30; F-30

* * * *

Require more and more eye contact from the client. Start by requiring the client to maintain eye contact momentarily when responding to the therapist at the beginning of the music therapy session. M-33

| B-5 | Demanding and intrusive (overly assertive) with staff (e.g., States that needs must be met immediately) (n3 = 0; n4 = 3; n5 = 3; 5.45%) |

During the music therapy session, have a discussion of personal boundaries and social appropriateness. For example, during music listening-discussion, elicit client feedback on appropriate ways to confront peers. F-35; F-60

* * * *

During music therapy, have the clients discuss and role play appropriate and reasonable ways to make requests. F-35

| B-6 | Uses passive dependent, passive aggressive, or aggressive methods of communication rather than being appropriately assertive (n3 = 0; n4 = 3; n5 = 3; 5.45%) |

Play the game, "Question Ball." The patients pass a ball to recorded or live background music. When the music stops the patient selects a question, reads it aloud, then answers the question. F-30

* * * *

During song writing, have the patients decide on the topic to be reflected by the title, then the title of the song. When composing the song, ask each patient to contribute one or two lines of lyrics/music to the song. F-30

* * * *

Employ assertiveness training techniques combined with various music activities and tasks. F-15

| B-7 | Lacks self-control; loses temper which may result in tantrums, violence, or arguments with other residents; low frustration tolerance; easily agitated when schedule is disrupted (n3 = 2; n4 = 1; n5 = 3; 5.45%) |

Involve the client in progressive muscle relaxation to music. M-30-25

Use relaxation exercises involving deep breathing while listening to music. F-35

B-8 Exhibits assaultive behavior (n3 = 1; n4 = 1; n5 = 3; 5.45%)

Have the client freely express anger through the playing of music instruments. Follow-up by having the client discuss verbally the reasons for the anger and appropriate solutions. The goal is to get the client to experience and acknowledge the gratification from using socially acceptable ways to express feelings. M-30; F-30

B-9 Development and channeling of creativity (n3 = 1; n4 = 1; n5 = 2; 3.64%)

Involve client in music expression activities using Orff techniques. M-30; F-30

B-10 Exhibits rocking behavior while seated (n3 = 1; n4 = 1; n5 = 2; 3.64%)

Conducting standing exercises to music. M-21; F-21

B-11 Complaining behavior (n3 = 1; n4 = 1; n5 = 2; 3.64%)

Utilize a music listening activity in which the client chooses his favorite music for listening. Follow-up with a discussion of what the client likes about the music. Ignore complaints and reinforce noncomplaints. M-21; F-21

B-12 Exhibits general perseverative behaviors (n3 = 1; n4 = 0; n5 = 1; 1.82%)

Utilize success-assured performance tasks such as autoharp strumming. M-30

B-13 Exhibits restless behavior; may have akathisia (n3 = 1; n4 = 0; n5 = 1; 1.82%)

Utilize music and movement activities such as structured dancing. M-30

B-14 Patient, age 50, complains about being in a session with younger patients in their early twenties (n3 = 1; n4 = 0; n5 = 1; 1.82%)

Encourage the older patient to choose music to play for the group, then explain to the group why they like the music. Encourage positive interactions among the clients. M-31

AFFECT (Combined, $n = 121$; 22.37%; Male, $n1 = 60$; 74.29%; Female, $n2 = 61$; 75.61%)

<u>PROBLEM</u>   <u>MUSIC THERAPY INTERVENTION</u>

A-1   Experiences difficulty, or the inability to verbally or nonverbally express/ identify feelings/ emotions in self or others (e.g., anger; happiness; sadness); difficulty understanding what the other person's feelings may be; restricted emotional expression; lack of congruity between affect and verbalization (e.g., facial expression, vocal tone and volume doesn't match speech content); may exhibit flat affect; emotional detachment; rarely smiles; may acknowledge own inability to experience feelings ($n3 = 28$; $n4 = 32$; $n5 = 60$; 49.59%)

Involve the client in a song discussion activity, focusing on the affective quality of the song (e.g., Ask the client: "Is this a happy, sad, angry, or fearful song?"). Use songs about specific emotions, such as fear, to help the client identify and express specific feelings and appropriate ways of expressing them. Prompt generalization to client's life situation. The overall goal is for the client to understand and accept feelings as a part of life. M-30-15-25-32-30-30;   F-65-41-36-30-15-37-35-31-26

Provide the patients with a list of mood states from the Hevner Mood Wheel. Have the patients listen to music, then select the specific mood which best matches the music. F-32

Use high intensity music for listening, followed by a discussion of feeling in the music. Later associate the feeling in the music to bodily sensation, and then to actual feelings within the client which are representative of the feelings in the music. F-35

Use music listening, pictures, and imagery to assist the client in identifying specific feelings elicited by the music. Ask the client to write any thoughts, feelings, or ideas that emerge while listening to music. Follow-up with a group discussion of written material. M-15-35; F-15

Perform different songs with an emotional theme, label the emotion, then discuss situations in the hospital where patients might feel the same. M-26

Have the client to bring songs to the session that express specific feelings related to issues the client is dealing with during hospitalization. Discuss feelings connected to the songs. M-41; F-41

Ask the client bring a song to the group, share the music with the group, then discuss/verbalize her feelings and memories associated with the song, and reasons for sharing the song. F-39

Ask the clients to pick a song which describes how they feel today. Attempt to elicit the feeling by playing the song. Encourage the clients to "act their feelings" (express their feelings) when talking with the group members. If expression of feeling is not forthcoming, ask the patients to draw their feeling while listening to the song. F-65 -31

Encourage clients to verbalize their feelings about songs after they are played, or to identify the feelings of the composer. Use this discussion as a catalyst for focusing on the feelings clients have about their problems. M-25; F-39

* * * *

During free or structured improvisation, prompt the client to identify feelings elicited by the improvisation. The client may be provided with a checklist of possible feelings to assist in the identification of own feelings. M-30-32;   F-30-35-39

Have a patient play an emotion on an instrument while the other group members, given visual and aural cues, guess what the emotion is. M-25

From a list of emotions (a "feeling list"), have the client express musically, with various instruments, each emotion on the list to achieve catharsis. M-51; F-51

Ask the client to select an emotion from a deck of index cards, each with the name of an emotion. The client first expresses the emotion using a musical instrument, and then verbally. M-35; F-32

Have the patient play and draw their feelings. Follow-up with a discussion of possible nonmusical outlets for expressing feelings. F-39

Ask the patient to choose an instrument or instruments from many (i.e. piano, tone bells, Orff xylophone, or other instruments). Have the patient express how she feels by playing the instrument(s). Follow-up by discussing the feelings with the patient. F-56-35

During rhythmic improvisation, ask the client to play on an instrument of her choice, her present feeling. The group is then asked if they can identify the client's feelings. Finally, the client is asked to verbally describe her feeling to the group. F-60

* * * *

Utilize voice lessons to develop expression of feelings. M-30; F-60

Ask the patient to choose a song (may be from a list of songs or a song book) that expresses his own feelings or describes himself to the group. The group will then sing and discuss the song. M-33-35-26; F-26-30

Involve the client in a choir in which the client chooses songs that convey feelings associated with happiness, sadness, death, and relationships. Have the choir sing and discuss such feelings. F-20

Sing songs such as "If You're Happy and You Know It." Follow-up with role playing of happy, funny, or sad situations/times. M-21; F-21

* * * *

Utilize song writing (e.g., The client portrays an emotion with an instrument such as a drum; the client expresses own emotions or feelings) M-25-30-60

Utilize a "Blues" writing activity. Patients write "feeling" phrases that may be sung with guitar accompaniment to a 12-bar blues pattern (e.g., "When I'm feelin' _____, I _____."). M-30

* * * *

Elicit client participation in music activity of client's choice while attempting to build a more trusting relationship with the client. M-45

Present the patient with a box containing labels describing positive emotions. Ask the patient to draw a label from the box, then tell about the time he experienced the emotion described on the label. This technique is useful with patients who experience difficulty talking about past positive life events. M-33

* * * *

The client chooses a song that describes his/her feelings. While the song is played, the client uses the group members to construct (nonverbally) a tableau (sculpture) which shows how he/she is feeling. The client then explains the tableau. M-35; F-65

A-2   Difficulty or the inability to identify or express emotions regarding a particular life situation; exhibits emotional detachment from life situations (e.g., denies being angry or having worries), (n3 = 3; n4 = 5; n5 = 8; 6.61%)

Use lyric listening to selected music and guided imagery techniques to give the client experience at associating and recognizing the emotions which accompany life experience. M-30-30; F-41-36-31

Have the patient choose a song which relates to one problem area in her life. F-50

* * * *

Adapt a song writing activity to facilitate the identification and expression of emotions associated with the life situation. M-51; F-51

A-3   Client becomes angry when coping with frustration; has difficulty coping with frustration or controlling resulting anger; experiences anger, stress, and frustration which may result in impulsive behavior; verbally hostile when frustrated (n3 = 6; n4 = 2; n5 = 8; 6.61%)

Implement relaxation techniques to diffuse anger. M-75

Ask the client to select, from a listing of song titles that express frustration, a title that best describes his own feelings. M-35-30; F-32

* * * *

Teach the client a new musical skill. Give the client experience at breaking down musical tasks into small steps which are more easily attainable. Facilitate client's generalization of this organizational principle (breaking down tasks) to the client's life situation. M-30-40; F-30

* * * *

Encourage the client to channel feelings into more constructive outlets, such as participating in a music activity (e.g., a performing group). M-75

* * * *

Utilize a variety of techniques: listen to song lyrics about anger; have the patient draw a picture of anger; ask the client to write a list of anything/anyone who makes him angry; encourage the patient discuss

anger with the group, share coping strategies, and receive
feedback (e.g., new ways to cope with anger). M-35

A-4   Hyperactivity; exhibits excitability behaviors; excessive energy levels;
agitation; manic behavior (e.g., excessive talking, waving arms) during manic stage
($n3 = 4$; $n4 = 2$; $n5 = 6$; 4.96%)

Utilize group singing with song sheets to elicit behavior which is
incompatible with excitatory behavior. M-21; F-21

Utilize singing or singing during structured dances to channel energy.
Use patient preferred music of medium tempo with many lyrics. M-40

* * * *

Utilize the iso-rhythmic principle; vector toward relaxing music.
M-45-30;   F-60

A-5   Depression associated with decreased energy level; has difficulty engaging in
tasks because of depression/ anhedonia; may only recall sad experiences; expresses
hopelessness; pessimistic about future ($n3 = 3$; $n4 = 3$; $n5 = 6$; 4.96%)

Utilize success assured tasks such as the client selecting records to share
with others, or asking the client to choose a song he likes. M-30

Involve the client in a small group (not all depressed patients) music
listening-discussion session. Use music that is of a moderate tempo (not
too slow or "upbeat"), and encourage clients to share their musical
interests and experiences. M-40; F-50

Have the client choose a song that describes how she feels, and one
describing how she would like to feel (e.g., the client expresses a
hopeless, pessimistic feeling, but would like to feel more optimistic about
her future). Discuss thoughts, actions, and other factors that may result
in feeling more optimistic. F-30

* * * *

Provide positive experiences through individual or group singing. F-50

Ask the patient to choose a song that she sang when she was young. After
singing the song, ask the patient to "share with the group" (tell about) a
special childhood friend. F-50

* * * *

Utilizing a variable speed record player, involve the client in simple stretching to music, followed by simple movement to a faster tempo. Use a song such as "Lake Song" from the motion picture, On Golden Pond. M-26

A-6   Severe depression accompanied by fear of real and imagined events; exhibits sad affect and states a desire to die; suicidal ideation; depressed affect; may exhibit loud, wild, screaming and crying (n3 = 4; n4 = 2; n5 = 6; 4.96%)

Ask the client to listen to music (recorded or live) and to experience the feelings she believes to be overwhelming. Utilize the group for support, and in the discussion of survival and coping strategies. F-39

Elicit positive statements or gestures from client during selected music listening activity. M-30

Listen to and discuss the song, "Don't Give Up." Help client relate to present life situation (e.g., severe depression; suicidal ideation). M-35

* * * *

Involve the client in the singing of familiar songs with a focus on validating own current emotions. F-25

* * * *

Provide the client with positive experiences at group instrumental performance or group singing. M-40

* * * *

Involve the group in the playing of musical games to elicit positive group affect (the goal is to get the depressed client to also experience the positive affect). F-25

* * * *

Assist client in developing the ability to concentrate on musical involvement to the exclusion, at least temporarily, of disturbing thoughts. M-40

> **A-7**   Free floating anxiety; not relaxed; easily frustrated; reports high level of anxiety about life situation; inability to relax; may be evidenced by muscle rigidity, sleep disturbance, verbal fretting, or verbal rumination (n3 = 3; n4 = 1; n5 = 4; 3.31%)

Utilize relaxation with music. Encourage the client to relax while listening. M-25

Schedule the client for water relaxation whereby floatation and music are combined. M-75

Teach appropriate relaxation procedures which patients can use outside of treatment groups. M-39

* * * *

Incorporate breathing and muscle relaxation exercises into vocal music instruction. Present progressively slower tempos to aid body-mind relaxation. F-35

> **A-8**   Impulsive emotional outbursts such as inappropriate laughing, crying, or anger; behavior may become unmanageable during periods of frustration; lacks self control or impulse control (n3 = 3; n4 = 1; n5 = 4; 3.31%)

Involve the client in a structured rhythm stick activity to rhythmic, stimulative music (e.g., Use the song, "Beat It."). M-30; F-30

* * * *

Choose musical conditions which serve as outlets for the expression of more socially acceptable behavior. Channel the energy into a music activity and control for inappropriate behavior. M-45; F-26

* * * *

Involve the client in progressive muscle relaxation to music. F-30

* * * *

Ask the client if the response is related to the musical experience; direct the client to the musical task. M-32

> **A-9**   Panic attacks (n3 = 2; n4 = 2; n5 = 4; 3.31%)

Music is utilized in a listening and/or imagery experience to aid in helping the client to learn relaxation techniques. M-41; F-41

* * * *

Instill a conditioned relaxation response to aid management of panic attacks. M-51; F-51

A-10 Angry emotional outbursts often resulting in violence; may be diagnosed as intermittent explosive disorder; short temper tantrums sometimes resulting in violence; difficulty responding to verbal feedback without becoming explosive/hostile towards self or others (n3 = 0; n4 = 3; n5 = 3; 2.48%)

During the music therapy session, encourage the patient to express intense feelings while maintaining control. F-35

Play Phil Collins' "I Don't Care Anymore." Discuss the client's anger. Have the client write two lists, one listing ways the client presently copes with anger, and the other listing healthier ways to deal with anger. F-65

* * * *

Redirect the behavior before it escalates (e.g., offer to let the patient listen to music through the Walkman; conduct music relaxation activities). F-25

A-11 Client feels emotionally "out of control" when listening to certain songs (n3 = 1; n4 = 1; n5 = 2; 1.65%)

Songs evoking "scary" or "out of control" feelings should be explored with the therapist. Discuss and explore songs, feelings, and issues related to the songs. M-41; F-41

A-12 Difficulty identifying and expressing own feelings which are perceived as being unacceptable (i.e. anger or fear); inability or difficulty recognizing suppressed feelings (n3 = 2; n4 = 0; n5 = 2; 1.65%)

Song discussions using carefully selected music which represents the patient's latent emotions. Observe for identification and projection. M-40

* * * *

Use referential improvisations on poignant subjects with subsequent discussion. M-40

A-13 Client experiences anger when the focus of attention is on other clients (n3 = 0; n4 = 1; n5 = 1; 00.83%)

Sing and discuss songs about sharing and noticing the needs of others.
M-33

A-14 Displays affect which is inappropriate to the situation (n3 = 1; n4 = 0; n5 = 1; 00.83%)

Have the patient improvise a sound pattern then verbalize the expressed emotion. F-32

A-15 Intellectualizes feelings (n3 = 0; n4 = 1; n5 = 1; 00.83%)

During lyric analysis, after listening to a selection, ask the client to identify the feelings expressed in the lyrics. Next ask the client to associate these feelings with similar feelings she is experiencing in the present, or has experienced in the past. F-60

A-16 Inability or unwillingness to empathize with others (n3 = 1; n4 = 0; n5 = 1; 00.83%)

A patient selects a three by five inch card from a set of "emotion cards," then improvises the emotion indicated on the card. Another patient is asked to attempt to identify the emotion from the improvisation, and explain why the first patient chose the particular emotion. M-40

A-17 Alternates between manic and depressive episodes; exhibits behavioral extremes (n3 = 0; n4 = 1; n5 = 1; 00.83%)

Redirect by involving the patient in expressive music activities such as song writing and improvisation. Use sedative or stimulative music.
F-37

A-18 Difficulty relating to staff that is the same sex as the abuser (e.g., female resents male staff) (n3 = 0; n4 = 1; n5 = 1; 00.83%)

Provide individual music lessons from a therapist who is the same sex as the abuser. Gradually explore the client's feelings as an alliance is established. F-31

A-19 Patient feels severe rage at mother for not providing protection during times of abuse ($n3 = 0$; $n4 = 1$; $n5 = 1$; 00.83%)

Involve the patient in a choir led by a female music therapist to give the patient experience at working with a female authority figure. F-31

SENSORY (Combined, $n = 20$; 3.70%; Male, $n1 = 10$; 50.00%; Female, $n2 = 10$; 50.00%)

<u>PROBLEM</u>   <u>MUSIC THERAPY INTERVENTION</u>

S-1   Client is preoccupied with internal thoughts; hallucinates; auditory hallucinations (e.g., hears voices); talks to ones self ($n3 = 3$; $n4 = 6$; $n5 = 9$; 45.00%)

Play patient preferred music during a listening-discussion activity. Redirect the patient's attention from internal events to interacting in group discussion about the music. Suggested discussion topics may focus on the music content, or patient ratings of the song. M-40; F-30

During listening-discussion group give the client experience at focusing on and distinguishing between internal and external stimuli. F-35

* * * *

Encourage on-task behavior in a music group (e.g., singing). M-25; F-26

Have the client follow song lyrics by singing, reading, or listening to music in a small group. F-30

* * * *

Utilize concrete, task oriented activities (e.g., playing, strumming, or pushing chords on the autoharp, or playing/improvising on other instruments) to assist the client in focusing on one task at a time. M-30; F-60-32

S-2   Client experiences difficulty coping with stress and tension; may result in insomnia, withdrawal, chaotic behavior, aggression, isolating self; refusing medications, substance abuse and/or other inappropriate behavior ($n3 = 7$; $n4 = 4$; $n5 = 11$; 55.00%)

Combine music with progressive relaxation techniques and guided imagery. Follow-up with a discussion of stress and methods of coping. M-15-30-30;   F-39-30-15

Encourage the client to attend a relaxation group which focuses on progressive muscle relaxation and breathing exercises. Follow-up with a statement from the client as to the level of relaxation achieved. M-75

Teach progressive muscle relaxation using music to elicit the responses. M-30

Use music listening combined with muscle relaxation. Use music agreed upon by the patient and the therapists. M-40

* * * *

Use lyric discussions to help facilitate problem solving of adequate, successful coping skills. M-15; F-15

IMAGERY (Combined, $n = 2$; 00.37%; Male, $n1 = 2$; 100.00%; Female, $n2 = 0$; 00.00%)

PROBLEM   MUSIC THERAPY INTERVENTION

IM-1 Difficulty envisioning a pleasant place during progressive relaxation ($n3 = 1$; $n4 = 0$; $n5 = 1$; 50.00%)

Have the client get comfortably situated then play background music. Ask the client, "What do you picture when listening to this music selection?" M-30

IM-2 Difficulty focusing on pleasant place for 10-15 minutes ($n3 = 1$; $n4 = 0$; $n5 = 1$; 50.00%)

Have the client watch a videotape of his attempted relaxation. Analyze the tape for any aural and/or visual clues as to why the client is having difficulty. M-30

IM-3   Distorted body image (associated with eating disorder) (n3 = 0; n4 = 1; n5 = 1;   50.00%)

Use music with progressive muscle relaxation to help the patient develop body awareness, or a realistic body image. F-31

COGNITIVE (Combined, n = 112; 20.70%; Male, n1 = 45; 40.18%; Female, n2 = 67; 59.82%)

PROBLEM   MUSIC THERAPY INTERVENTION

C-1   Low self esteem; reports feelings of worthlessness; expresses low opinion of self; makes negative self statements; exhibits problems talking to others because of low self esteem; has difficulty expressing positive aspects about self; lacks the necessary self-confidence to try to overcome life problems or to try new activities; convinced they are destined for failure; may feel they have no special skills, or that they can't do anything meaningful; discounts compliments (n3 = 10; n4 = 20; n5 = 30; 26.79%)

Utilize instrumental or vocal music therapy activities to produce a positive experience either individually or in a group. Utilize success oriented music activities to enhance self esteem (e.g., playing the Omnichord; encourage instrumental experimentation and improvisation). Engineer the instrumental performance to produce client feelings of success, accomplishment, and peer acceptance. M-30-51-25-25; F-30-51-39-39-60

Teach the client to play a musical instrument (e.g., guitar or piano) or give voice lessons (depending upon capabilities). During lessons, have the client point out at least one positive aspect of their playing. M-35-30; F-41-32-65-60

* * * *

Involve client in lyric analysis-discussion activities. M-40; F-50-39

Have patients listen to and choose songs about positive self statements. As a follow-up, have each patient construct a list of positive self statements to keep with them, and to review when they start thinking negative statements about themselves (e.g., Use the song, "Desiderata" to explore positive aspects of self). M-26; F-26-39

Play Billy Joel's, "Just the Way You Are." Discuss the idea of accepting yourself as you are. Ask each client to "List on a piece of paper, three things you like about yourself." Have the clients pass their papers around the group so each group member can add something else they like about each client. F-65

Have the patient choose a song title that represents her. F-28

* * * *

Involve the client in song composition activities. M-35; F-50

Arrange for the client to learn a new skill such as song writing. M-40

* * * *

Have the client draw to selected music. Follow-up with interpretation and discussion. F-41-50

* * * *

Play musical games which require paired teams such as "Music Pictionary." F-50

* * * *

Have the patient make an album cover that represents her. F-28

C-2   Delusions; expresses delusional ideas; paranoid ideation (e.g., patient accuses the therapist of saying things against the patient); has difficulty accepting reality; may perceive actions of others as potential threats; excessively concerned with protecting one's own interest; does not trust peers (n3 = 5; n4 = 9; n5 = 14; 12.50%)

Redirect discussion to reality oriented statements (e.g., ask the patient to identify the names of instruments or the performer in a music recording). M-30; F-32

Utilize a music listening-discussion session in which the client is encouraged to sit with the other group members. Encourage the client to talk about and choose music that makes them feel more comfortable towards others. F-20

Involve the client in a lyric discussion group with the eventual goal of the client sharing her own music with the group. F-39

Play a song about concrete concepts (e.g., "This Land Is Your Land"). During the discussion probe for reality statements from the client (e.g., Where were you born?; When were you born?; What is your present address?). M-26; F-26

During music-listening, arrange for the client to get group feedback concerning ideas in a song which are similar to ideas in the client's delusions. M-25

* * * *

Discuss why certain topics of discussion for social situations and settings are appropriate or inappropriate. Involve the client in various social uses of music, such as background music for discussion and dancing. F-30

Involve client in activities such as social mirroring dances and musical charades. M-35

Arrange for the client to experience trust. Using a recording of the song, "Lean on Me," have the clients form a circle, hold hands, then lean back so that the group supports each other's weight. F-30

* * * *

Sing songs with lyrics that reinforce positive self esteem. M-35; F-30

* * * *

Redirect the client's focus to concentrating on a musical project. Getting the client involved in playing an instrument, if interested, is especially effective at redirecting delusional conversation. F-37

* * * *

During music therapy session do activities which require sharing and trusting. F-37

C-3   Lacks problem solving skills; inability to view alternatives to problems; inappropriate coping mechanisms (drinking, drug abuse, verbal/physical aggression; feeling overwhelmed); difficulty organizing tasks; difficulty identifying logical steps toward accomplishing a goal; may view problems as being unmanageable; lacks insight; has difficulty managing problems occurring both on the hospital unit and outside the hospital ($n3 = 4$; $n4 = 9$; $n5 = 13$; 11.61%)

Involve the client in lyric analysis and song writing activities. Prompt the client to find solutions to problems reflected in the song lyrics, the patients life, or both. Employ role reversal techniques. M-40; F-50-26-28

After singing the song, "Gonna Lay Down My Burdens," have the patients identify a burden (problem) they are experiencing, and at least one step they can take toward a resolution. Re-write into the song all the information gained about burdens and their resolutions. F-39

Utilizing Blues form, write a Blues song allowing patients to vent in the first verse their frustrations over unsolved problems. Follow-up with a discussion about how to solve the problems and cope with the frustration. Write the resulting solutions and coping mechanisms into the second verse of the song. F-39

Cut each staff line from a piece of sheet music (complete song). Mix up the pieces of paper, each containing a staff line, then ask the client to reassemble or reconstruct the music so the therapist can use the music to sing the song. F-56

*   *   *   *

Using a song such as "Bridge over Troubled Waters," have the group identify problems they have experienced, and various ways they have coped with the problems. F-39

During music listening-discussion, have the patient identify both appropriate and inappropriate coping skills heard in songs. M-40

Select the song, "Logical Song" by Super Tramp for listening-discussion. Ask the patients to identify a goal and draw a road map which shows how they will achieve the goal. F-56

Play Twila Paris', "The Warrior Is a Child." Have the patients draw a personal shield. On the shield, have the patients draw/list things they have in their life that help to provide them with motivation. F-65

Implement stress management and relaxation techniques. M-35

*   *   *   *

Observe the client's ability to obey rules during group improvisation (e.g., "Only one person can play at a time."). M-40

C-4   Disorientation; difficulty with orientation (person, place, and time), memory/ attention span; lacks reality orientation; loose associations; may be caused by physical illness such as Organic Brain Syndrome or Alzheimer's disease ($n3 = 5$; $n4 = 7$; $n5 = 12$; 10.71%)

Utilize song discussion (after singing or listening to a familiar song) to encourage the client to express specific reality oriented statements (e.g., about past or present events). Redirect inappropriate responses.
M-41-32-30;   F-41-60

* * * *

Utilize musical games such as "Name That Tune," or filling in the blank (missing lyric) on song sheets. F-31-30

Play the game, "Question Ball." The patients pass a ball to recorded or live background music. When the music stops the patient selects a question, reads it aloud, then answers the question (This activity may need to be adapted to the functioning level of the client). F-30

* * * *

Complete a questionnaire on the client's musical preferences (part of the music therapy assessment). Perform a simple arrangement of a popular song (e.g., "The Rose") on the metallophones. Ask the client to play a "C" and say his name, or play a "G" and say his neighbor's name. M-26

Involve the client in an activity which requires reality oriented behavior, such as playing instruments in rhythm and with correct chords. Elicit appropriate comments and maintain on-task behavior.
F-41

* * * *

Involve the client in a very structured activity, such as drawing to music. M-35

C-5   Exhibits poor short/long term memory skills; difficulty remembering names ($n3 = 2$; $n4 = 3$; $n5 = 5$; 4.46%)

Ask the patient to identify their music preferences during a sing-a-long activity. Follow-up by performing the preferred songs. F-32

After the client finishes singing a song, ask the client to recall the name of the song. M-30

Have the patient recall music patterns, such as the rhythm or the melody, during the session. M-32

* * * *

Practice short-term recall by asking the patient questions about the song lyrics. F-41

* * * *

Ask the client to name each instrument used in a given improvisation session. F-25

C-6	Poor decision-making skills; may have difficulty making daily life decisions or recognizing own erroneous decisions (n3 = 2; n4 = 3; n5 = 5; 4.46%)

During the music therapy session have the client select from among two o r more instruments, which instrument he will play. M-32

Ask the patient to orchestrate and lead a small group improvisation based on a selected title card (e.g., "Rain Storm"). M-40

* * * *

Given a list of songs ask the client to choose one song for group singing. Also, given two favorite songs, the client must choose one for group singing. F-31

* * * *

Given a tape recording containing various songs, have the client select one song for listening and discussion. The lyrics of the song must describe a coping skill. F-60

* * * *

Have the patient choose from a variety of activities such as instrumental, vocal, or listening, and from materials associated with such activities (e.g., tapes; songs; instruments). F-35

C-7	Client denies having problems; withdraws from problems; exhibits resistance to treatment during therapy or hospitalization (n3 = 3; n4 = 1; n5 = 4; 3.57%)

Discuss song lyrics that relate to the client's problems; choose songs for lyric analysis that focus the client on specific therapeutic issues. M-30-41; F-30

* * * *

Provide a relaxed/nonthreatening music experience (e.g., learning the guitar; music listening) to encourage trust and increase personal insight through gentle redirection by the therapist. M-41

C-8   Client has difficulty accepting responsibility for change; has difficulty accepting change in basic daily routine (n3 = 2; n4 = 1; n5 = 3; 2.68%)

Employ structured improvisation (e.g., on the song "La Bamba") followed by the changing of instruments (regardless of the client's choice of instrument). Follow-up with a discussion relating to change. M-26

Involve the client in a success-oriented, very structured music therapy activity (e.g., Orff instrumental activity). Gradually increase client responsibility and change variables as the client feels more comfortable with the group. M-35; F-32

C-9   Gives up easily when solving problems; easily frustrated; inability to cope with failure; goes to bed upon not being successful (n3 = 1; n4 = 2; n5 = 3; 2.68%)

Involve the client in a dyadic improvisation with the music therapist. The patient selects a three by five card instructing him to, in some manner, change the improvisation of the therapist. Observe frustration threshold. M-40

Teach the client a music performance skill. Insure a reasonable amount of success, but remind the client that all persons make mistakes when learning to play a music instrument. Generalize principle to real life situations. F-50

* * * *

Have a discussion of song lyrics which pertain to the relationship between perseverance and success. F-30

C-10   Difficulty following directions; inability or unwillingness to listen to or comprehend directions (n3 = 0; n4 = 3; n5 = 3; 2.68%)

Demonstrate a music task to the client (e.g., how to play a tambourine). As the client's ability to follow directions improves, increase the task complexity (e.g., teach one rhythm pattern, then two rhythm patterns, etc.) F-32

During instrumental improvisation, give the client simple one or two step directions about how to play a percussion instrument. F-25

* * * *

Make group rules and directions for music activities exceptionally clear and easy to understand. F-37

C-11 Client is unaware of the purpose or need for hospitalization; may be resistive to treatment (n3 = 1; n4 = 1; n5 = 2; 1.79%)

Encourage client discussion of personal needs during reflective song discussion groups. M-35

* * * *

Provide a relaxed, nonthreatening music experience (e.g., learning guitar; listening) to encourage trust and increase personal insights through gentle redirection by the therapist. F-41

C-12 Client has difficulty accepting or coping with the reality of hospitalization; may feel hopeless and discouraged (n3 = 0; n4 = 2; n5 = 2; 1.79%)

Have the group members compose a parody to the song, "Please Release Me." F-30

* * * *

Have the group listen to the song, "There's a Place in the Sun." Follow-up with a discussion of what gives them encouragement, and how they can find additional sources of encouragement. F-30

C-13 Client admits own problems, but denies others may have similar problems (n3 = 1; n4 = 1; n5 = 2; 1.79%)

Involve the client in a lyric analysis discussion about general life problems and ways to cope with them. M-35; F-32

C-14 Client experiences difficulties with verbal therapy because of low level of functioning (e.g., chronic disorder) (n3 = 1; n4 = 1; n5 = 2; 1.79%)

Involve the client in rhythmic activities (e.g., playing rhythm instruments to accompany songs) to elicit physical involvement and organization of thoughts. M-41; F-41

C-15   Delusions of grandeur (e.g., unrealistic aspirations to be a "rock star"); maintains delusional system regarding self as a famous musician (n3 = 0; n4 = 2; n5 = 2; 1.79%)

For unrealistic "rock star" aspirations, involve the client in reading and discussing biographies of musical performers, especially "rock stars." Follow-up by assigning musical tasks according to ability. F-37

*   *   *   *

Use a gradual progression of activities, beginning with involving the client in playing/singing, then audio taping the client, and next videotaping the client. The goal is to confront the client's delusional system, while fostering a more realistic client perception of actual skills and abilities. Reinforce and develop the client's real strengths. F-35

C-16   Demonstrates poor judgment; difficulty assessing social situations and following appropriate protocol (n3 = 2; n4 = 0; n5 = 2; 1.79%)

Following the discussion of a musical style preferred by the group, ask the client to select, from a variety of styles, music to which the group would like to listen. M-32

*   *   *   *

Ask the client to supply the appropriate solution (i.e., "Fill in the blank") to a variety of problematic social situations. M-40

C-17   Lack of self-awareness (n3 = 1; n4 = 0; n5 = 1; 00.89%)

Involve client in music relaxation and discussion to help client become more aware of present life situation. M-35

C-18   Difficulty with setting goals (n3 = 1; n4 = 0; n5 = 1; 00.89%)

Involve the client in a goal sharing group. The clients listen to goal-related songs, then each client writes a time line for future specific goals. M-30

C-19   Misinterprets messages/communications from others (n3 = 0; n4 = 1; n5 = 1; 00.89%)

Use instruments to role play conversations, arguments, conflicts, or other personal experiences. Discuss client perceptions of the type of communication that took place during the improvisations (e.g., angry conversation?; casual conversation?; was the conflict settled?). F-39

C-20   Feelings of helplessness ($n3 = 1$; $n4 = 0$; $n5 = 1$; 00.89%)

Involve the client in a reflective discussion of song lyrics which
relate to the client's problem. M-35

C-21   Lacks ability to structure time, manage a limited budget, and utilize
community resources ($n3 = 1$; $n4 = 0$; $n5 = 1$; 00.89%)

Conduct group singing of songs about efficient community living. Follow-
up with group discussion. M-25

C-22   Difficulty or inability to relate to metaphor ($n3 = 1$; $n4 = 0$; $n5 = 1$;
00.89%)

During song discussion, encourage the patient to explain own
interpretation of the lyrical metaphor used in the song. M-40

C-23   Lacks concept of a healthy heterosexual relationship; becomes involved in
destructive relationships resulting in emotional and physical abuse ($n3 = 0$;
$n4 = 1$; $n5 = 1$; 00.89%)

Conduct lyric discussions of songs having themes related to the client's
problems (e.g., intimacy; loneliness; dependency; friendship; support).
F-35

INTERPERSONAL-SOCIALIZATION(Combined, $n = 177$; 32.72%;
Male, $n1 = 96$; 54.24% %; Female, $n2 = 81$; 45.76 %) Includes LEISURE SKILLS

<u>PROBLEM</u>   <u>MUSIC THERAPY INTERVENTION</u>

IS-1   Reclusive; withdrawn; isolative behavior; minimal personal interactions;
does not feel comfortable or relate to others when in group; little or no
verbalization; may not initiate conversation; may be preoccupied with personal
problems or depressed ($n3 = 28$; $n4 = 34$; $n5 = 62$; 35.28%)

Involve the client in music listening and discussion of the lyrics, artist,
or other musical characteristics. Wait for the client to respond.
M-25-30-21-32-31;   F-30-21-39

Utilize a record selection activity, where patients are paired off and asked
to select a song to which they both can relate. Although the activity goal is
to facilitate peer interaction, group discussion may also be facilitated.
M-30-25

Involve the group in writing a story about the group which is set to instrumental background music, with the goal of facilitating verbalization and interaction. M-51; F-51

Ask the client to collaborate with his neighbor in determining five singers whom they both like. M-33; F-30

Tape a piece of paper on each client's back. Play the song, "That's What Friends Are for," then have each client write on the back of each client, one positive quality about the client. M-35; F-32

After listening to songs such as, "You've Got A Friend," "That's What Friends Are for," and "There's a Winner in You," the client must state a positive quality about the peer seated on the right, the left, and herself. F-60

Involve the client in a group music therapy session in which each client picks a record that describes herself, then tells the group why. F-20

As an exercise in negotiating skills, ask the patients to choose, from a stack of 10 albums, only two songs for listening. M-85

Establish initial participation by presenting a music activity in which the client is interested. Follow-up by gradually involving the client in music listening-discussion of musical selections significant to the client's problems. M-45

To promote the sharing of music experiences, assign each patient to bring to the session the music of their favorite artist, and give a presentation to the rest of the group. M-80

Choose music for discussion which describes positive qualities possessed by all group members. F-60

*   *   *   *

Give one-to-one instrumental instruction to establish rapport and trust. Prepare the client for participation in a music ensemble, or to play a solo, with the goal of increasing interpersonal interaction. F-36-31-31

Play "Stop the Music." The clients pass a rhythm instrument around the group while the music plays. When the music stops, the client holding the instrument chooses a card from the "grab bag." The client reads the card to the person on his left, who in turn must answer the question. M-21; F-56-21

Present group improvisation on a variety of instruments, letting patients take turns directing. The director indicates through hand positions what the group is to do (e.g., get louder, higher, or lower). During the following discussion, present questions such as, "What does it feel like to be in front of people, or to be a leader?" "How did you communicate?" "Do we ever need to change our communication techniques?" F-31-26

Arrange the conditions in a music performance group so clients must listen to other performers in order to match pitches and rhythms. F-37

Conduct structured improvisation without verbal interaction (i.e., begin with having the client mimic an answer/response). F-35

Select an improvisation activity requiring the patient to choose a partner, or one in which two clients play simultaneously. M-40

Create an improvisation using two xylophones. Instruct two group members to have a "conversation" using only the instruments to "talk." Follow-up with a discussion of the interaction. F-39

Place the resident in a performing group. Encourage interaction and conversation with other residents. M-25

Ask the client to choose a group member to trade instruments with, and to name the group member. F-25

*   *   *   *

Involve the client in group singing with an emphasis on cooperative interpersonal interaction. M-51-25

During group singing, promote client recall of the names of group members. Songs which require the greeting or naming of peers may be used. M-30; F-30

Ask the client to collaborate with her neighbor in choosing a song for the group to sing. F-26

During the music therapy session, have the client introduce their peers or neighbor and tell something about them. Facilitator songs may be used such as "Getting to Know You." F-35

During a talent show or sing-a-long arrange conditions for client interaction (e.g., sharing song books; sharing microphone; singing with peers). F-35

*   *   *   *

Play the following game: Arrange the group in a circle and have the group members throw a ball to whoever they wish while the music plays. When the music stops, the person holding the ball must tell something good about the person who threw the ball. M-21; F-21

Encourage group interaction by involving the client in musical games (e.g., "Pictionary;" "Musical Bingo"). F-28

Facilitate structured interaction through musical games (e.g., Music Trivia; a dice game). F-65

* * * *

Involve the client in movement/dance activities. M-35-40

Develop nonverbal interaction skills by having the client participate in mirroring to music. F-26

Introduce a music and movement task with defined space limitations (i.e. the client must remain in the circle or square). M-32

* * * *

During song composition, compose parodies (rewriting the lyrics of familiar songs) to describe each group member (e.g., name; feeling) or on group themes. Sing the parodies during group singing. F-35-30

Utilizing a song writing activity (e.g., fill in the blanks technique), assist the patient in identifying a hierarchy of social activities, perceived by the patient from least to most threatening. Have the patient make one hierarchy for hospital and one for community social activities. M-40

Each client will write a poem, read the poem aloud to the group, and then orchestrate the poem. Encourage group members to volunteer to play instruments and to assist where needed. F-39

* * * *

Conduct structured interviews to determine musical interests. Appoint partners with similar interests to share their interests with the group. M-26; F-26

* * * *

Have the patient design an album cover complete with art work and song titles that describe her. Upon completion, the patient is asked to show the finished album to the group and talk about it. F-56

Arrange for the patients to work on a project together, such as putting together a display featuring various music groups. M-85

* * * *

Build self-esteem through positive musical experiences. M-30

* * * *

Encourage the client to attend a small music variety group (two-four members), and participate in activities such as group singing, rhythm band, and informal "jam" sessions. During the activities, encourage the client to respond to the therapist's questions. M-75

* * * *

Use music activities which encourage the patients to make non-intimidating contact with one another (e.g., physical contact; verbal contact; eye contact). F-35

IS-2 Does not utilize leisure time; has difficulty constructively managing or structuring leisure time; indicates a lack of "things to do;" frequently does nothing, sleeps, or watches television; poor leisure skills; lacks leisure skills; no hobbies or interests ($n3 = 20$; $n4 = 12$; $n5 = 32$; 18.08%)

Demonstrate different styles of music to find out the client's likes and dislikes. Provide 20-30 minutes each day for listening. Reinforce behavior. M-21-30; F-21

Provide leisure education about community activities and music as leisure. Take the client on field trips to community music events such as concerts and recitals. M-35; F-36-30

Develop healthy ways of structuring free time by taking clients on field trips to community events such as concerts, plays and museums. M-30

Teach the client to pursue personal music interests, such as providing training on how to buy a stereo and build a tape library. M-30; F-30

Use guided imagery and music to help the patient explore leisure interests. M-26; F-26

Ask patient to express leisure interests/skills by drawing to music.
M-26;   F-26

* * * *

Develop music performance skills such as piano or guitar playing for use as leisure after discharge. Have the patient compile a notebook of songs and chords learned. Arrange performance opportunities for the client.   M-30-25-25-26-75-40-30-30;   F-60-30-31

* * * *

Teach the client a musical skill which can be used in the community (e.g., singing in the church choir). M-30; F-50-26

Have the patient construct a "leisure collage" by looking through magazines and cutting out pictures of leisure activities. Sing related songs such as "My Favorite Things." F-35

* * * *

Teach music theory to the patient if some music performance abilities are present. M-26

Assist the client in composing a song, then publish the song in the hospital newsletter. M-40

* * * *

Start with simple stretching activities to music, then progress to dance (e.g., Country and Western; Rock; Polka). M-31

* * * *

Prepare the client for re-entry into the community by explaining community music recreational opportunities. Prepare client for participation. M-45

IS-3 Uncooperative behavior in group settings; uncooperative with staff and patients; disruptive; breaks rules; interrupts; does not change behavior to conform to rules; chooses to not follow directions (n3 = 8; n4 = 9; n5 = 17; 9.61%)

Involve the client in group singing to enhance cooperative interpersonal interaction. F-51

Involve the client in a music "combo" activity such as a choir. Cultivate group awareness and cohesion. M-30-40-30-30; F-30

* * * *

Using resonator bells or tone chimes, assign a bell to each group member. Emphasize the importance of following directions and working together to achieve the final product. M-35-40; F-35-32

Pair patients into groups of two or more. Ask them to plan, practice, and perform a music selection, with each taking a turn at playing a solo while the other members of the instrumental group accompany. F-32

*   *   *   *

First work with the client on a one-to-one basis to prepare for integration into a music ensemble. M-30; F-60

*   *   *   *

Involve the client in a music activity of choice with as much individual attention as possible. If the uncooperative behavior does not improve, remove the patient from the group for one week. F-37

When planning a music therapy activity, involve the client in the formulation of "reasonable" rules for the activity. F-37

*   *   *   *

Ask the client to work with another client in assigning a rating (1 through 10) to a selection of music. F-25

*   *   *   *

Involve the client in musical team games such as Music Trivia, Music Bingo, and Musical Chairs. M-40

IS-4 Lack of interest and motivation to use leisure time; is not motivated to engage in leisure activities; boredom resulting from a lack of interests; may choose watching television/ smoking as only leisure activities; has limited leisure skills; has few friends ($n_3 = 8$; $n_4 = 5$; $n_5 = 13$; 7.36%)

Utilize music listening activities to identify musical interests and to increase motivation to use music as leisure. M-30; F-30

Refer the client to a listening laboratory in which he can accumulate points for each 20 minutes of music listening. Points can then be exchanged for numerous items (excluding cigarettes). M-21; F-21

Utilize music listening activities to teach the patient about music they may enjoy. Incorporate group discussion to stimulate verbal interaction with peers. M-31

Improve musical skills to develop interests in music leisure activities. Give the client the opportunity to discover past skills or to use existing skills. One approach may be to use lyric analysis to discuss types of music skills, with the goal of remotivating the client to use such skills. M-35-40;   F-50

* * * *

Involve the client in leisure music activities that would prepare the client for musical opportunities in her home town, such as square dancing, theatrical groups, or social dances. F-20

Use music passively as background music to nonmusic recreational activities, such as physical exercise, walking, and lifting weights. F-35

* * * *

Search out possible musical experiences from past life and develop. If none are found, introduce new ones that are easy to acquire. M-45

Assist client in discovering musical interests and in developing the use of music as leisure. M-30

* * * *

Conduct an instrumental improvisation session on the client's ward. M-25

IS-5 Experiences difficulty in bonding with others as evidenced by lack of friendships and/or excessive marital conflicts; difficulty maintaining long term (more than one year) relationships/friendships; difficulty relating to or feeling comfortable with others (n3 = 1; n4 = 4; n5 = 5; 2.83%)

Utilize group singing to integrate the patient into the "patient community bond." M-15; F-15

* * * *

Utilize movement games which require interaction with others (e.g., imitation of the movement of others). F-50

* * * *

During group improvisation, give the client experience at both leading and following. F-50

* * * *

Conduct a listening-discussion session of songs that focus on positive aspects of relationships/friendships. Follow-up by having the clients improvise on instruments the feelings they associate with relationships/friendships. F-35

IS-6 Experiences difficulty with the sharing of personal data, such as likes and dislikes with the group; has difficulty with, or is withdrawn from disclosing personal issues (n3 = 2; n4 = 3; n5 = 5; 2.83%)

After a session in which the patient has disclosed personal issues to the group, sing a bonding song such as "Amazing Grace." M-15; F-15

* * * *

Have the client bring songs to the session that express specific feelings related to issues the client is dealing with during hospitalization. Discuss the feelings. F-41

* * * *

During rhythmic improvisation the client selects a peer group member with whom she needs to share information (e.g., personal issue; problem; concern), but is unable to do so verbally. The client then shares and exchanges information nonverbally with the peer, each using instrumental improvisation. After the improvisation the client discusses the information with the peer. F-60

* * * *

Use musical games to help make information sharing nonthreatening to the client. M-15

IS-7 Has difficulty involving self in community groups; unable to make acquaintances in church or community (n3 = 3; n4 = 1; n5 = 4; 2.26%)

Teach the client the expectations of a community choir, and develop vocal performance skills. M-30; F-30

Prepare the patient to join a church choir by giving voice lessons and self confidence training. M-33

Conduct group singing and discussion of songs about friendship and positive relationships. M-25

IS-8 Does not sit with group; sits near the periphery of the group; sits behind group members or alone; continually leaves the room, or stands and watches the group from afar (n3 = 3; n4 = 1; n5 = 4; 2.26%)

Use rhythmic improvisation. Encourage the client to select an instrument and to participate in ensemble playing with group members. Although the client may initially remain seated near the periphery of the group while playing, as the client feels more comfortable, encourage her to assume a more central seating position in the group. F-60

* * * *

Play music, then ask each individual in the group to say something about the person next to them. M-31

* * * *

Make choosing a favorite song contingent upon sitting with peers. M-33

* * * *

Involve the client in small group discussions, in which all members of the group are encouraged to participate. Suggested topics may focus on the clients themselves, family, work, or future goals. M-31

IS-9 Inappropriate relationships with the opposite sex; inappropriate remarks about sexual topics; asks inappropriate personal questions (n3 = 3; n4 = 1; n5 = 4; 2.26%)

Involve the client in a coeducational square dance activity with emphasis on appropriate heterosexual interaction (e.g., appropriate touching and verbalization). M-30-40; F-30

* * * *

Involve the client in listening-discussion of songs such as "Getting to Know You." Discuss appropriate questions and topics for interactions with females. M-40

IS-10 Self centeredness; client has difficulty listening to the problems of others; becomes impatient when sharing attention with other clients (n3 = 1; n4 = 2; n5 = 3; 1.70%)

Have each client select a song that best describes how they feel. The therapist elicits discussion and feedback from the group members. M-35; F-32

Ask the patient to think of a group member who is interested in people other than him/herself, then select a song which describes the group member. F-30

IS-11 Client is a loaner who frequently says undesirable things about other clients and staff (n3 = 2; n4 = 1; n5 = 3; 1.70%)

The therapist leads the group in writing lyrics to a familiar song. Each client must say three nice things about the person on his right. The therapist incorporates the three nice things into the song. M-21; F-21

* * * *

The therapist reads the lyrics then plays the song, "Just the Way You Are." Follow-up with a discussion about accepting others in the group. M-35

IS-12 Wears clothing inappropriate for the occasion (n3 = 1; n4 = 1; n5 = 2; 1.13%)

Make attendance at special music programs contingent upon appropriate dress. M-30; F-30

IS-13 Egocentric, childish behavior (e.g., refuses to take turns or to share); does not work well with group (n3 = 2; n4 = 0; n5 = 2; 1.13%)

Present music conditions in which the client must work and get along with peers. The goal is to foster client insight into the value of cooperative behavior by having the client experience the greater benefit of peer acceptance, as opposed to the peer rejection associated with always having one's own way. M-45

The therapist will introduce a "mystery song." The clients will subsequently play the song in a tone bell ensemble in a cooperative effort to identify the song. M-25

IS-14 Excessive and inappropriate verbalization (e.g., individual is loud and continually talks during the session) (n3 = 1; n4 = 1; n5 = 2; 1.13%)

Arrange conditions to give the client experience at taking turns talking. For example, let each client in the group take turns picking out the recording of a song, playing their song for the group, then explaining to the group why they like the song. M-31; F-25

IS-15 Attention seeking (n3 = 1; n4 = 1; n5 = 2; 1.13%)

Involve the client in a rhythm activity which emphasizes group cooperation rather than individual attention. M-30; F-30

IS-16 Client exhibits poor group leadership and organizational skills. (n3 = 1; n4 = 1; n5 = 2; 1.13%)

Have the client score a "sound symphony" (percussion instruments) titled "Who Am I." The client, using the other group members as performers, will then conduct the symphony. M-35

* * * *

During group music therapy, provide each group member with the opportunity to lead the group in creative movement to music. F-32

IS-17 Patient frequents barrooms during leisure time; lacks healthy leisure time activities (n3 = 1; n4 = 1; n5 = 2; 1.13%)

Involve the patient in guitar lessons and encourage him to practice during free time. M-33

* * * *

Give clients an orientation to community activities through field trips to community events such as concerts, plays, and museums. F-30

IS-18 Demonstrates a lack of awareness of others (n3 = 1; n4 = 0; n5 = 1; 00.57%)

Utilize a hand bell performance group (one note per client) to emphasize working with peers. M-30

IS-19 Difficulty learning names; does not bother to learn the names of persons who bear a close, long term relationship with the patient. (n3 = 0; n4 = 1; n5 = 1; 00.57%)

During music composition, write songs which include the names of the group members and their characteristics. F-28

IS-20 Has difficulty tolerating small groups (n3 = 1; n4 = 0; n5 = 1; 00.57%)

Invite the client to join the group. Once in the group, give the client more freedom of choice (e.g., where he sits or which song to sing). M-26

IS-21 Inappropriate relationships with the opposite sex; excessively flirtatious towards male peers ($n3 = 0$; $n4 = 1$; $n5 = 1$; 00.57%)

> Involve the client in structured music therapy sessions (e.g. dance) that teach the client how to talk with peers without flirting. F-20

IS-22 Aggressive and manipulative ($n3 = 1$; $n4 = 0$; $n5 = 1$; 00.57%)

> Present client-preferred music activities in which mutual consideration and cooperation is required for the success of the activity. M-45

IS-23 Lacks knowledge of how to have fun in a nondestructive manner ($n3 = 1$; $n4 = 0$; $n5 = 1$; 00.57%)

> Utilize music (e.g., Music Trivia) and nonmusic games to develop on task socialization, frustration tolerance, and positive leisure activities. M-25

IS-24 Exhibits appropriate behavior at community events ($n3 = 1$; $n4 = 0$; $n5 = 1$; 00.57%)

> Take the patients on an outing to a concert in the community. M-85

IS-25 Argues frequently with authority figures ($n3 = 1$; $n4 = 0$; $n5 = 1$; 00.57%)

> Involve the patient in drum lessons to sublimate aggression. Also, give the patient experience at relating to leaders in nonthreatening music activities such as chorus and group singing. M-30

IS-26 Interacts with staff but not with peers ($n3 = 0$; $n4 = 1$; $n5 = 1$; 00.57%)

> Announce that each client is going to have to tell something to the group about their neighbor. In the presence of background music, allow each client to interact with their neighbor about what is to be told. When the music stops, each client then tells something about their neighbor. F-20

IS-27 Client becomes impatient and intolerant when another client chooses a song he doesn't like ($n3 = 1$; $n4 = 0$; $n5 = 1$; 00.57%)

> Have clients choose songs they would like someone else in the group to hear. Discuss the musical characteristics of the song (e.g., dynamics) and the message of the song. M-33

IS-28 Does not participate in leisure activities because of excessive working (e.g., "workaholic") (n3 = 1; n4 = 0; n5 = 1; 00.57%)

Involve the client in a music exercise group to help develop relaxation techniques. Inform the client of places that have exercise programs to use after the client leaves the hospital. M-31

IS-29 Does not participate in leisure activities because they increase stress (n3 = 1; n4 = 0; n5 = 1; 00.57%)

Use a sing-along with songs that identify feelings or leisure activities which reduce stress (e.g., "Bicycle Built for Two"). M-30

IS-30 Client is withdrawn and passive during one-to-one session with therapist (n3 = 1; n4 = 0; n5 = 1; 00.57%)

Utilize improvisation as a means for individual expression and in nonverbal dialogue with the therapist to increase the client's awareness of self in relation to others. M-41; F-41

IS-31 Client stays in bed all day (n3 = 1; n4 = 0; n5 = 1; 00.57%)

Conduct activities on the client's ward that he may be attracted to, or that might lure him out of bed. Utilize the client's favorite music in such activities. M-25

IS-32 Client will not attend group (n3 = 1; n4 = 0; n5 = 1; 00.57%)

Find any special interest in music; agree to play the client's favorite song. M-25

DRUGS (Combined, n = 54; 9.98%; Male, n1 = 23; 42.59%; Female, n2 = 31; 57.41%

Includes:

D-1.0 SUBSTANCE USE OR ABUSE and MEDICATIONS, Combined, n = 18; 3.33 %; Male, n1 = 8; 44.44%; Female, n2 = 10; 55.56%)

D-2.0 PHYSICAL WELL BEING (Combined, n = 15; 2.77%; Male, n1 = 5; 33.33%; Female, n2 = 10; 66.67%)

D-3.0 PHYSICAL COMMUNICATION PROBLEMS (Combined, n = 21; 3.88%; Male, n1 = 10; 47.62%; Female, n2 = 11; 52.38%)

<u>PROBLEM</u>   <u>MUSIC THERAPY INTERVENTION</u>

D-1.1 Engages in substance abuse during leisure time; may drink excessively and frequently at local barroom or at home (n3 = 2; n4 = 3; n5 = 5; 27.78%)

Play barroom music (if client preferred), then have clients discuss the music. The discussion may focus on a lyric/music analysis including whether the lyrics were valid/ the meaning or message of the song. M - 3 1

Use lyrics of songs that reflect upon the client's use of alcohol. Have the client to verbalize what their life was like before the alcohol abuse and what it is like now. Give the client a lyric sheet and ask her to listen to the song. F-20

Choose songs for lyric analysis that focus on alcoholism and other addictive problems. F-35

* * * *

Provide instrumental instruction to develop appropriate leisure interests and as an alternative to substance abuse. M-51; F-51

D-1.2 Client denies having a substance abuse problem (n3 = 2; n4 = 2; n5 = 4; 16.67%)

From a list of 150 song titles, have the patient select five which relate to themselves. Follow-up with a listening-discussion session. F-56

During music discussion group, use music with lyrics portraying substance problems. (e.g., "Alcohol," the Kinks; "Life in the Fast Lane," the Eagles; "The Pusher Man," Steppen Wolf)This activity may provide a nonthreatening condition for assisting the client in stating how their problems relate to those in the music. M-31

The client is given a list of 50 song titles and asked to make two lists of 10 titles each. One list of songs should describe their addiction, and the other list should describe their recovery up to the present. Both lists should show the progression of the addiction and recovery. F-60

Play an appropriate song such as Amy Grant's, "Don't Run Away." Follow-up with a discussion of life problems the client may be "running from." M-31

D-1.3 Client attributes substance abuse to life stress; uses substances for relaxation ($n3 = 2$; $n4 = 1$; $n5 = 3$; 16.67%)

Develop a strategy for reducing stress. Use music relaxation as an alternative to managing stress. Conduct music listening sessions which focus on relaxation with light imagery. Have the client listen to the music (tapes), imagine a pleasant place, then focus on how he feels afterwards. M-25-30; F-65

D-1.4 Client lacks awareness of how the pattern of substance abuse has progressed; may be unaware of lost leisure or vocational skills, or lost values. ($n3 = 1$; $n4 = 2$; $n5 = 3$; 16.67%)

Through drawing a record album cover and writing original titles, the patient will describe how life was before treatment, during treatment, and goals for the future. M-85

* * * *

Teach the client leisure activities which can be done without the use of drugs. For example, involve the client in a music exercise class. Focus on increasing self-esteem, self-worth and self-image. F-20

* * * *

The client is given a list of ten song titles which can be thought of in terms of values (e.g., values regarding cocaine, friends, faith, etc.). The client then classifies the values under either "addiction" or "recovery." Follow-up with a discussion of healthy values. F-60

D-1.5 Client is reluctant to discuss substance abuse and treatment issues ($n3 = 1$; $n4 = 0$; $n5 = 1$; 5.56%)

Ask the client to bring a song which describes his addiction. M-85

D-1.6 Manipulates the environment to get their own way, sometimes by being dishonest; may experience guilt. (n3 = 1; n4 = 0; n5 = 1; 5.56%)

Choose songs for lyric analysis that focus on alcoholism and other addictive problems. F-35

D-1.7 Inability to identify coping mechanisms, rehabilitation goals, or to solve problems associated with self-defeating addictive behavior (n3 = 0; n4 = 1; n5 = 1; 5.56%)

Utilizing two lists, each containing 20 song titles, ask the client to write two short stories. One story, written from the first list, is to describe the client's own addiction, and the other story, written from the second list, is to describe the client's recovery. The client is to incorporate actual song titles into the context of the sentences. F-60

D-1.8 Mourns loss of drug habit (n3 = 0; n4 = 1; n5 = 1; 5.56%)

Use song writing and discussion to help the patient through the mourning. F-31

D-2.1 Absence of daily exercise routine; poor muscle tone (n3 = 1; n4 = 1; n5 = 2; 13.33%)

Involve client in 20-minute rhythmic exercise routine with prompts, five days per week, or as prescribed. M-30; F-25

D-2.2 Poor personal hygiene (n3 = 1; n4 = 1; n5 = 2; 13.33%)

Make client's favorite music activity (such as access to the piano or stereo) contingent upon daily bathing. M-30; F-30

D-2.3 Insomnia (n3 = 1; n4 = 1; n5 = 2; 13.33%)

Formulate and record a music/relaxation program for the patient to use PRN (as needed) to decrease insomnia. M-51; F-51

D-2.4 Lack of neuromuscular endurance in upper extremities (n3 = 0; n4 = 1; n5 = 1; 6.67%)

During group improvisation, have the patient to improvise five to ten minutes on a variety of percussion instruments. F-25

D-2.5 Poor gross and fine motor coordination (n3 = 0; n4 = 1; n5 = 1; 6.67%)

Assess and treat through various types of music activities (e.g., instrumental lessons; movement to music) F-15

D-2.6 Poor eye-hand coordination (sensory integrative functioning) (n3 = 1; n4 = 1; n5 = 2; 13.33%)

During instrumental music improvisation, require the client to strike the mallet in the center of the xylophone bars. M-30

* * * *

Play the game, "Balloon Toss to Music." Seat the clients in a circle, play some "fun" background music, then ask the clients to take turns "hitting the balloon" to another client. Because balloons move slowly, this activity allows for delayed reactions characteristic of some clients (e.g., geriatrics). F-30

D-2.6 Vestibular problems (sensory integrative functioning) (n3 = 1; n4 = 1; n5 = 2; 13.33%)

Involve the client in folk dances which require bending, twisting, and changing directions. See: Schoreder, Block, and Campbell, *Adult Psychiatric Sensory Integration Standardized Assessment* (an occupational therapy assessment). M-26

For problems with vestibular input, use popular dances to give the patient practice at going under the arm of their partner (e.g., two-step Country and Western; part of the Jitterbug). F-31

D-2.6 Lack of proprioceptive feedback (sensory integrative functioning) (n3 = 1; n4 = 0; n5 = 1; 6.67%)

Assess the client's ability to perceive the beat of the music (See Weikart, *Teaching Movement and Dance*, High/Scope Press, Ypsilanti, MI). Client performs rhythmic patting to the music first with the hands, then the feet, then by walking to the beat. M-26

D-2.7 Lacks spatial awareness; unaware of position of body in space (sensorimotor) (n3 = 0; n4 = 1; n5 = 1; 6.67%)

Involve the patient in structured dance (e.g., Have a circle dance in which the patients line up holding hands, go backwards 8 to 16 counts, then forward to the starting position). F-31

> **D-2.8** Lack of diaphragmatic control (from excessive purging associated with eating disorder) ($n3 = 0$; $n4 = 1$; $n5 = 1$; 6.67%)

During choir or individual voice lessons, use vocal exercises that focus on appropriate use of the diaphragm. F-31

> **D-3.1** Difficulty or inability to verbally communicate with others; unable to maintain conversation; poor communication skills; poor quality of communication during interactions; doesn't communicate coherently; slurs speech; experiences difficulty being understood ($n3 = 5$; $n4 = 6$; $n5 = 11$; 52.38%)

Conduct nonverbal musical call and response activities with the client (e.g., Therapist plays a musical antecedent at the piano and the client responds with a musical consequent). M-30

Encourage the client to sing song lyrics coherently, with good diction. F-25

In a one-to-one session, have the client sing their thoughts. Gradually expand the song content to permit the client to tell a complete story. F-20

Have the clients sing and chant familiar song lyrics. F-32

* * * *

Given Orff instruments, have two patients use the instruments to carry on a conversation with each other. M-30; F-30

Ask the client to respond musically (nonverbally) on an instrument with the therapist (e.g., during improvisation, the client solos while the therapist accompanies, or vice versa). F-25

* * * *

Have clients pass a ball while listening to music. When the music pauses, the client with the ball verbally responds to a question. M-30

* * * *

Use musical games that focus on basic communication skills. M-15; F-15

* * * *

Conduct a "fill in the blank" song writing activity. M-50

* * * *

Utilize the tape recorder as an assessment and treatment tool. Tape record the patients speech, let the patient listen to the tape recording, formulate and implement speech goals, then evaluate by recording a second time, the patient's speech. F-28

D-3.2 Poor nonverbal communication (inappropriate eye contact, affect, and gestures) (n3 = 2; n4 = 1; n5 = 3; 14.29%)

Have the client use nonverbal communication techniques to direct group Orff improvisation activities. M-30; F-30

Involve the client in nonverbal conversation by playing music instruments. The music instruments are utilized as the nonverbal communication tool and are played in a "call and response" format. Follow-up activity with a discussion of appropriate nonverbal cues and communications. M-25

D-3.3 Responds to questions with one word sentences (n3 = 1; n4 = 1; n5 = 2; 9.52%)

During lyric analysis and discussion, have the patient describe what the lyrics mean. M-35; F-32

D-3.4 Exhibits pressured speech (n3 = 1; n4 = 1; n5 = 2; 9.52%)

Use vocal techniques and slow tempi to elicit a slower rate of speaking and more distinct enunciation. M-45; F-37

D-3.5 Client attempts to communicate but makes irrelevant comments about the topic being discussed (n3 = 1; n4 = 0; n5 = 1; 4.76%)

During music discussion, redirect client statements by asking questions related to the topic of the particular lyric analysis. M-31

D-3.6 Poor breath support/control (n3 = 1; n4 = 0; n5 = 1; 4.76%)

Involve the patient in appropriate music therapy activities such as voice or piano lessons. M-15

D-3.7 Client speaks too softly to be heard (n3 = 0; n4 = 1; n5 = 1; 4.76%)

Have the client select a song for the group to sing, then loud enough for the group to hear, tell the group the name of the selected song. M-33; F-30

CODE: N = Total number of music therapy interventions submitted for Adults.

N1 = Number of music therapy interventions submitted for adult males for all assessment areas. % = Percentage of N

N2 = Number of music therapy interventions submitted for adult females. % = Percentage of N

n = Total number of music therapy interventions submitted for a particular area of assessment. % = Percentage of N.

n1 = Number of music therapy interventions submitted for males within a particular area of assessment. % = Percentage of n.

n2 = Number of music therapy interventions submitted for females within a particular area of assessment. % = Percentage of n.

n3 = Number of music therapy interventions submitted for males for a particular problem. % = Percentage of n5.

n4 = Number of music therapy interventions submitted for females for a particular problem. % = Percentage of n5.

n5 = Total number of music therapy interventions submitted for the particular problem. % = Percentage of n.

* * * * = Separates different types of music therapy interventions (e.g., playing instruments; singing; composing; moving to music; specified behavior modification techniques; other).

Number(s) after each intervention (e.g., 36) refers to the mean **Global Assessment of Functioning Scale** (*GAF Scale*) score of the clients for whom the intervention is designed. One score was given by each music therapist specifying the intervention (e.g., "25-30-36" indicates that the particular intervention was submitted by three music therapists, and that the intervention is used with clients having the above mean *GAF* scores).

PSYCHIATRIC MUSIC THERAPY ASSESSMENTS AND TREATMENTS EMPLOYED IN NAMT-APPROVED CLINICAL TRAINING FACILITIES: ADOLESCENTS (N = 156)

ASSESSMENT AREA

BEHAVIOR (n = 11; 7.05%)

PROBLEM   MUSIC THERAPY INTERVENTION

B-1   Lack of assertiveness; unaware of nonverbal, nonassertive body language projected; does not exercise basic classroom rights, obligations, or responsibilities (e.g., the right to think for ones self; the freedom to make mistakes while learning; risking one's opinion); does not state own needs or desires (n1 = 5; 45.45%)

Give each client a choice of songs to sing or instrument to play. Each client must make a selection/decision. 50

Involve the client in group/individual improvisation on a preferred instrument. 40

* * * *

Involve the client in solving cooperation puzzles by using nonverbal communication. 46

* * * *

Have the client choose three song titles to be used in confronting oneself, and in confronting a peer on either side of oneself. 50

* * * *

Role play and compare assertive, aggressive, and passive behavior during group music activities (activities such as creating music, playing instruments, moving to music, and listening to music). 40

B-2   Attention deficit disorder; lack of attention span; attends to tasks only for short durations; lack of concentration (n1 = 3; 27.27%)

Engage client for longer periods of time during music activity (e.g., Plays musical composition for longer periods of time without stopping). 50

Give individual music lessons. Structure five minute breaks during the practice time. 31

*   *   *   *

Have the client participate in an art project while listening to a favorite song (e.g. cover a long conference table with a sheet of paper and have the group to participate in the drawing of a mural). 36

B-3	Withdraws from social situations ($n1 = 1$; 9.09%)

Involve the client in musical drama. Assign the client a roll which is comfortable and which the client can tolerate. 36

B-4	Hyperactive; unable to focus ($n1 = 1$; 9.09%)

Encourage the client to focus on one task (e.g., During music lessons, have the client to focus on one song and one instrument. During choir have the client focus on one song). 31

B-5	Inability or unwillingness to follow staff directions ($n1 = 1$; 9.09%)

Make participation in a socially valued music group contingent upon cooperation with the unit medical teams. 45

AFFECT ($n = 51$; 32.69%)

PROBLEM	MUSIC THERAPY INTERVENTION

A-1	Inability to identify/express feelings; states "I don't know" when asked how she or others feel; flat or inappropriate affect; lack of congruity between affect and verbalization (e.g., facial expression, body posture/language, vocal tone and volume doesn't match speech content) ($n1 = 17$; 33.33%)

Have the patient identify feelings expressed by the singer/song writer in popular song lyrics. 46-50-50

Conduct a "feeling card" activity in which the patient, given a number of cards, selects the card with the word that matches the feeling projected in the music (e.g., frustration). 46-46

Have the patient bring to the "Music Issues Group," a musical recording which relates to feelings or thoughts about issues chosen by the group for discussion. Encourage the patient to appropriately participate in the discussion. 31

During group discussion, have the client to identify specific feelings or emotions expressed in popular song lyrics. 31

Ask the client to bring a favorite song to the session, play it for the group, discuss the meaning of the lyrics, and explain why the lyrics are meaningful to the client. 36

Have the client listen to instrumental music and identify her own feeling state. 40

Give the client a list of feelings and ask the client to choose a song which parallels a feeling from the list. 50

Lay out pictures of faces which project different emotions. Play music which generates strong emotion. Have the patient choose the picture which best represents the emotional quality of the music. Follow-up with a discussion of the picture, the music, and the emotion. 43

*   *   *   *

Have the patient communicate their present feeling by improvising on an instrument. The patient also may use body language which appropriately expresses their feeling as they improvise (including role playing with instruments).   25-46

Have the patient express any feeling word nonverbally by improvising on rhythm instruments while using body posture representative of the feeling. In the following discussion ask the patient to relate a time when she felt that way. 40-50

*   *   *   *

During a song writing activity, have everyone focus on the theme, "Expressing Myself." 40

Use music composition based on the 12-bar blues pattern. Encourage patients to use lyrics which describe their feelings. 46

A-2 Exhibits anger or rage towards others; overly aggressive; may be destructive to self, others (yelling; fighting), or property (e.g., hitting walls; throwing chairs) ($n1 = 13$; 25.49%)

Ask the client to play the drums while maintaining the level of control necessary for maintaining the required tempo, dynamics and other musical characteristics. The goal is to practice maintaining control during periods of frustration, and to provide a constructive outlet for frustration, anger, and other intense emotions. 35-45

During group improvisation on rhythm instruments, ask the group to improvise the meaning of two opposite words (e.g., Improvise "peace," then improvise "chaos"). During group processing, ask the clients to focus on relating to one of the words. 50

Have the patients participate in nonverbal "conversations" with one another by improvising on xylophones or other rhythm instruments. 50

Redirect the patient's behavior toward an awareness of appropriate modes of expression. Begin by expanding the client's repertoire of emotional responses. For example, during a drum activity, ask the client to create different rhythms to signify different degrees of feeling/emotion. 35

Give the client experience at cooperating with other group members in the creation of a desirable musical performance (e.g., using resonator bells, have the clients improvise on the pentatonic scale). 35

List anger eliciting situations on a chalkboard (e.g., Your sister just broke your brand new compact disc player). Ask the patient to express on a rhythm instrument, how he/she would feel in the situation. Discuss appropriate solutions and the consequences of inappropriate solutions. 4 3

*   *   *   *

Have the patient select a song from an album to express the anger being felt. Follow-up by having the patient identify personal, appropriate alternatives for ventilating the anger. 50

Play two or three popular songs which relate to retaining anger, "blowing up," and appropriately asserting or expressing anger. Follow-up with a discussion of which technique of expression is most typical of the client. 50

Ask the patients to bring and share with the group their own "angry" music/songs. Have the patients rank their songs on a continuum of most to least angry. Also, have the patients to classify their music/songs as "contributors" to or "relievers" from anger. 50

*   *   *   *

Make participation in a socially valued music group contingent upon appropriate behavior (i.e., If inappropriate behavior occurs, revoke the patient's group membership for one or two weeks). 45

*   *   *   *

Using drama and music, have the student act out a stressor (precipitator), followed by positive (adaptive) physical, cognitive, and emotional reactions. Discuss with the student how these reactions felt. 40

* * * *

Have the client verbalize impulses related to own feelings, then explore alternative responses (e.g., Have the client to insert lyrics to a structured song which presents an alternative to the client's responses). 31

> **A-3**   Experiences stress reactions; may result in difficulties such as sleep disturbance, digestive disorders, anxiety, poor judgment, impulsive behavior, and faulty decision making; poor stress management skills; may interfere with the discussion of painful issues ($n1 = 7$; 13.73%)

Utilize guided imagery and music (GIM) activities to visualize successful involvement in stressful situations. Promote self awareness and insight. 50-46

Employ relaxation, or progressive muscle relaxation training utilizing media and techniques such as music, biofeedback, and video taping. Also use a stress level scale ranging from 1 to 10, and music relaxation with guided imagery. 31-46-43-50

* * * *

During discussion, assist the client in discovering acceptable and workable ways, which fit the patient's life style, to cope with stress (e.g., aerobics or other exercise to music; performing music). 31

> **A-4**   Experiences anxiety; may be over on-going problems, unresolved issues or feelings, internal conflicts, or upcoming event; the anxiety may be reality-based about events such as future placement or discipline; may result in sleep disturbance such as nightmares ($n1 = 4$; 7.84%)

Lead the patient in progressive muscle relaxation, and then in guided imagery. Have the patient imagine being in the anxiety-provoking situation, then imagine a positive outcome. Follow-up with a discussion of how the positive outcome can be a possibility. Encourage the patient to practice the imagery, and assist the patient in choosing background music. 40-50

* * * *

Develop the client's musical interests to, at least temporarily, replace the client's fears. The goal is to use music therapy as a distracter, thereby creating a palliative effect. 36

* * * *

Teach the patient to use the guitar to accompany breathing exercises (i.e. playing simple relaxing chord progressions, such as F Major 7 to C Major 7, to accompany slow, deep breathing). 46

A-5	Lacks self control; poor impulse control (n1 = 3; 5.88%)

Employ relaxation training with biofeedback, music response, and key word response. 31

* * * *

Give piano instruction. The goal is for the client to begin to experience the self-satisfaction and rewards of self control by learning to play the piano. 36

Reduce negative comments and sanctions from peers (which may trigger poor impulse control) by improving peer relationships. Involve the patient in a music performance group in which all must work collectively to portray a specific message through the performance (e.g., musical selections/improvisations representing trust and friendship). 36

A-6	Patient has difficulty identifying and verbally sharing feelings related to significant life experiences (e.g., trauma/fears) (n1 = 2; 3.92%)

Play a song having lyrics related to the patient's trauma/fears. After listening to the song, encourage the client to share, during group discussion, thoughts, feelings, and symbols that were elicited by the song. 2 5

* * * *

Establish patient trust in the music therapist; use song-writing and improvisation activities. 45

A-7	Depressed (n1 = 2; 3.92%)

During lyric analysis, assist clients in relating the lyrics to their personal lives. Ask the patients to identify similar problems in their lives, then discuss appropriate solutions. 51

* * * *

Give one-to-one musical instruction. The goal is to increase enthusiasm for life experiences, self confidence, and peer acceptance through the learning of a socially valued skill. 45

A-8	Suicidal (n1 = 1; 1.96%)

Ask the patients to bring and to share with the group their own "angry" or "depressing" music/songs. Have the patients rank their songs on a continuum of most to least depressing or angry. Also, have the patients classify their music/songs as "contributors" to, or "relievers" from depression or anger. 50

A-9	Patient has difficulty expressing positive feelings towards peers (n1 = 1; 1.96%)

Ask the patient to bring a recording that describes a positive relationship she has with a peer. 20

A-10	Expresses emotions in a variety of socially unacceptable ways (n1 = 1; 1.96%)

Use songs and improvisation to elicit intense emotions, such as anger and fear. 40

SENSORY (n = 0; 00.00%)

PROBLEM   MUSIC THERAPY INTERVENTION

IMAGERY (n = 1; 00.64%)

PROBLEM   MUSIC THERAPY INTERVENTION

IM-1	Distorted body image (associated with eating disorder) (n1 = 1)

Use music with progressive muscle relaxation to help the patient develop body awareness, or a realistic body image. 31

COGNITIVE (n = 32; 20.51%)

<u>PROBLEM</u>   <u>MUSIC THERAPY INTERVENTION</u>

C-1   Low self-esteem; low sense of values/personal importance causing dysfunctional interpersonal interactions; makes negative self statements; experiences feelings of worthlessness; lacks self-respect and self-confidence; may exhibit poor eye contact (n1 = 10; 31.25%)

Reduce negative comments and sanctions from peers (which may produce low self-esteem) by improving peer relationships. Involve the patient in a music performance group in which all must work collectively to portray a specific message through the performance (e.g., musical improvisations/songs representing trust and friendship). 36

Involve the patient in a performance group. Prepare a music performance to be given to peers, therapists, teachers, family, or other significant persons. 50

Give instrumental music instruction. Reinforce realistic musical goals while assisting the patient in identifying unrealistic goals. 46

Provide individualized music therapy sessions focused on learning to play an instrument or song writing. 40

Family involvement is crucial at the high school level. Invite families to musical performances to build self-esteem and to open doors to constructive communication (Respondent Note: The family has the greatest impact on students. Compared to the family, school and therapy are of secondary importance. The musical performance can be used as a nonthreatening way to involve families.) 50

Emphasize belief in oneself. Give credit to those who try. Help the student to understand there is some success in trying, no matter what the result. Give the students many opportunities to perform. Spare no effort to assure that those who perform are well received. 50

*   *   *   *

Perform one of the client's favorite songs on guitar or piano. Ask the client to listen to the song, then write a parody (new lyrics) of the song. 36

Assist each student in writing their own song. Arrange for each student to receive praise and recognition by playing each student's song at a public performance. 40

*   *   *   *

Focus on positive rather than negative aspects of behavior. Use individualized music activities which bring out a student's musical strengths. As musical strengths are developed, showcase them! 50

During music therapy, emphasize constructive measures (i.e., correct the behavior, not the child) (Heim Ginott philosophy). The musical/social behavior may need improvement, but the child is accepted unconditionally. 50

> **C-2**   Lacks problem solving skills; inability to identify a step-by-step procedure for resolving problems; fails to respond to problem solving cues; fails to recognize apparent solutions to problems; may feel overwhelmed and out of control of self or future ($n1$ = 4; 12.50%)

Use guided imagery and music relaxation. During guided imagery ask the patient to imagine problem situations and to mentally rehearse being in control. 43-46

* * * *

Involve the client in a tone bell ensemble. Provide the client with tone bell music (therapist constructed music indicating notes to be played and their location on the staff) and direct the group to perform the music. Provide positive reinforcement for correct performances (i.e., correct notes played). Follow-up with a discussion of processes necessary to the success of the activity. Relate to other life situations. 40

* * * *

Cut each staff line from a piece of sheet music (complete song), then place the resulting pieces of paper in an envelope. Give the envelope to the patient, asking her to reassemble or reconstruct the music so the therapist can use the music to sing the song. Assist the patient with musical notation and symbols, but encourage the patient to use problem solving cues inherent in the lyrics (e.g., Do the lyrics rhyme? Are the lyrics logical? Do the lyrics "make sense"?) 40

C-3   Gives up easily when solving problems; low frustration tolerance; resulting disappointments may lead to inappropriate behavior such as disruptive behavior ($n1 = 3$; 9.37%)

Involve the client in the group task of composing or creating a dance to a selected song. Encourage the group members to help one another learn the dance steps. All group members should be involved in the performance of the dance. 40

Involve the client in activities such as song writing and music improvisation to reduce frustration and inappropriate behavior. 36

* * * *

Present a music activity that requires learning a new skill (e.g., learning new rhythms on percussion instruments). Increase frustration tolerance. 50

C-4   Exhibits paranoid behavior; makes "mountains out of mole hills;" minor incidents considered a threat; does not trust others ($n1 = 2$; 6.25%)

Concentrate and redirect the patient's attention toward the musical task or activity. The goal is to channel the patient's energy into constructive outlets. 45

* * * *

Have the student participate in a guided imagery experience focused on the issue of trust. 40

C-5   Exhibits "narrow mindedness" causing misunderstandings; does not respond well to suggestions from others, or to constructive criticism ($n1 = 2$; 6.25%)

Conduct a story telling activity in which each group member tells a story after/while listening to nonverbal music. Follow-up with a discussion of the story content. 36

* * * *

Create compositions (e.g., music; poetry) based on story content derived from guided imagery and music activities. Have students critique the compositions of others; encourage students to accept constructive criticism. 40

| C-6 | Lacks awareness of, or insight into own personal problems (n1 = 2; 6.25%) |

During song writing, write a parody (lyric substitution) about changes that the client has made and needs to make. Follow-up with related discussion. 50

* * * *

Using songs reflective of the patient's problems, prompt the patient to relate own behavior, opinions, or problems to those presented in the song. 40

| C-7 | Poor organizational skills; impaired ability to organize, alphabetize, categorize, or file information or materials related to academic subjects, or school activities in general; inability to prioritize or set goals (n1 = 2; 6.25%) |

Have the students construct a music notebook in which they organize all the music information obtained during music therapy class time. 40

Assist students in establishing and prioritizing individual therapeutic goals which motivate and challenge them. It is very important that students be expected to follow through with (i.e., achieve, or make progress toward) their goals. During music therapy, place a major emphasis on the successful follow through of music goals to promote positive generalization to other behavior. 50

| C-8 | Poor conflict identification and resolution skills; experiences on-going conflict with parents (n1 = 2; 6.25%) |

Discuss music lyrics/ television Sit-Com situations. Stop the video taped Sit-Com at predetermined places for a discussion of alternative solutions to problem situations presented in the Sit-Com. Also discuss the reality of the solutions presented in the song lyrics/ Sit-Com as related to the patient's experiences. 31

Have the client listen to and discuss the songs, "Father and Son," or "Cats Cradle." Ask the patient to write a letter to the parent with whom there is a conflict, describing what the problem is and suggesting some alternatives ways to solve the problem. 40

| C-9 | Inability to cope with family conflicts (n1 = 1; 3.12%) |

Conduct improvisation with instruments, using the instruments to represent family members engaged in conversation, conflict, and other typical interactions. Follow-up with a discussion of conflict resolution techniques. 50

C-10 Lacks awareness of one's role in a family, or insight into own family interactions (n1 = 1; 3.12%)

Have the client improvise on rhythm instruments, with assistance from others, to show how her family interacts (e.g., appoint one performer to be mother, one to be father, until there is a performer for each member of the family. Improvise typical interactions and scenarios). 50

C-11 Lacks awareness of ones own relationship to peer group (n1 = 1; 3.12%)

Involve the group in the writing of a musical rap about both, the common and individual issues of each group member. 36

C-12 Does not trust therapist; will not honestly communicate with therapist (n1 = 1; 3.12%)

Trust is the key to success with those who are emotionally disturbed. Until honest communication occurs, there is little or no progress. Only when an emotionally disturbed student feels that you are genuinely there to help, will trust and honest communication occur. 50

C-13 Inability to make decisions; does not express preferences, needs, likes or dislikes (n1 = 1; 3.12%)

Involve the client in a listening or performance activity. Verbally give the client feedback about behavioral observations, such as, "I saw you smile and pat your foot during this song. It looked as though you liked it." 4 6

INTERPERSONAL-SOCIALIZATION (n = 49; 31.41%) (includes LEISURE SKILLS)

<u>PROBLEM</u>   <u>MUSIC THERAPY INTERVENTION</u>

IS-1 Uncooperative behavior; noncompliant with stated rules and limits; does not follow directions (e.g., "Stay in your chair;" "Stay on task;" "Work quietly;" "Be nice to others;" "Finish your work on time;" "Raise your hand before speaking"); refuses to take turns, share or to compromise; conduct disorder; exhibits inappropriate behavior both on and off hospital/school grounds (n1 = 13; 26.53%)

Involve the patient in an instrumental performance group. Assign responsibilities (e.g., musical roles) so each patient's cooperation is dependent upon group success. 51

Involve the client in activities that require the sharing of leadership (e.g., improvisation). 50

Involve the client in group improvisation activities. 40

During a xylophone improvisational activity give each client a tone bar. Ask the group to follow (imitate) the musical characteristics of the designated leader's improvisation (e.g., imitate dynamics and tempo). 35

During a drum activity, ask the clients to pass the drum around the group, and for each client to play a different rhythm. 35

* * * *

Involve the patient in a highly structured group musical game with contingent music listening as the reward for winners (e.g., Use musical games such as "Crosswords," lyric puzzles, and "Music Trivia" which focus on team work and cooperation). 40-50

Make attendance to music sessions (singing; listening to music; moving to music; creating music; playing instruments) contingent upon earning points in the "classroom discipline point system." 40

* * * *

Give the group a stack of recordings and ask them to choose two selections of music they would like to hear. 20

* * * *

Make attending a local performance or concert contingent upon appropriate behavior. 20

* * * *

Have the patients work together on a project such as a musical collage. 20

* * * *

Involve the patient in dance and rhythmic exercise groups which require listening to, and then following directions. 36

* * * *

Involve the student in lyric interpretation leading to a discussion of ineffective and effective coping techniques. 40

IS-2 Lacks awareness of self or others; detached; poor peer relationships; does not interact appropriately with peers (e.g., does not give or receive positive comments; excessively negative); lacks respect for others; has difficulty making friends; distances others through sarcasm, anger, and other destructive defenses (n1 = 12; 24.49%)

Involve the client in group rehearsals and the subsequent performance of a song. 40

During performance group, redirect client comments such as "I Like the way that sounds" to "(Client's name) played well." Discuss reactions of peers to positive/negative statements. 46

Provide experience at supporting others by involving the client in "supported solos" during group improvisation. The client will demonstrate the ability to both accompany other clients, and the ability to take solos while being accompanied. Monitor the client's ability to take both leader and follower roles. 50

* * * *

Do the activity, "song title Feedback Fan." Each client takes turns selecting a song title representative of each group member. The song titles are then assembled into the shape of a paper fan, and discussed with each group member. 50

Conduct lyric discussions about songs which identify (1) destructive defenses, and (2) positive self protection in relationships. 40

* * * *

Involve the client in activities which require working with group members towards common goals, or emphasizing or utilizing the strengths of each member (e.g., video projects involving music or drama). 31

Involve the client in group activities such as making a music video, putting on a radio show (e.g., interviewing), and music composition (song statement). 46

* * * *

Involve the client in group activities such as playing instruments, learning popular songs, lyric analysis with discussion, drawing to music, lyric writing, and music appreciation (contrasting popular artists). Emphasize appropriate interaction (e.g., appropriate language; taking turns; complimenting peers; positive self statements). 51-50

* * * *

Involve the client in writing and performing song parodies (re-writing lyrics), and in sharing information about each group member. 40

* * * *

Involve the patient in activities that provide unique individual attention such as a talent show. 36

* * * *

Involve the client in group music activities requiring interaction through touch, verbalization, and movement. 50

IS-3 Withdrawal; does not share thoughts, feelings, or interests; does not ask or answer questions; does not communicate with others; isolates self ($n1 = 9$; 18.37%)

During music listening, play music which was popular in past decades. Ask the students to identify the decade in which the music was popular, to identify the instrumentation, and to discuss societal issues which were prevalent when the music was popular (i.e. Discuss issues of the 1950's, '60's, '70's, and '80's after listening to music of the same era). 40

Ask students to contribute to history charts, or a music notebook, showing aspects of life in the 1950's, '60's, '70's, and '80's. Ask them to contribute recorded music, books, videos, and pictures. 40

Ask each group member to bring to the next session a recording of a favorite song, to play it for the group, and to briefly describe the music, the performer, and any other points of interest about the recording. 50

Ask the client to choose songs to play for the group which communicate messages to the group. After the group listens to the song, follow with a discussion and feedback about what the group heard communicated. 40

During "Music Exploration," ask the clients to bring information on a chosen music topic to the next meeting. At the next meeting, have the clients discuss the information they found on the music topic. Plan a community outing to observe the performance of the music (e.g., An example topic might be "Recorded Music." At the next session have the clients discuss how music is recorded and work on a group song to record. Plan to visit a recording studio and observe the studio musicians). 31

* * * *

Involve the group in the writing of a canon which uses names of the group members. Encourage the group members to work together so the canon can be performed successfully. 43

Have the clients express their own ideas by filling in the blanks when using a "fill in the blanks" music composition activity (e.g., the client completes open, or incomplete lyrical statements). 50

* * * *

Encourage group involvement by utilizing activities such as playing instruments, group singing, and musical games. Assign an individual part in a performance ensemble (per patient ability). Do not try to force conversation. Gradually add more discussion requirements. 31-46

> **IS-4** Inappropriately uses leisure time; lacks knowledge of community-based leisure activities available to students; spends leisure time with gangs ($n1 = 6$; 12.24%)

Give instruction in how to teach one's self to play a music instrument (e.g., guitar; keyboard). Give the necessary materials to the patient and check weekly for progress and questions. Encourage home practice. 31-46-40

Give music lessons; involve the patient in the school band or orchestra, or in other community activities. 46

* * * *

Expand music preferences to include a variety of styles. Musical preferences can be developed during music listening, music theory, and instrumental and vocal instruction. 46

* * * *

Expand knowledge of arts activities in the community; discuss arts events listed in the newspaper; take weekly field trips to arts events. 40

* * * *

Teach musical games, such as "Instrument Pictionary," "Name That Tune," and "Musical Bingo." 43

IS-5   Does not/lacks motivation to engage in leisure activities (n1 = 3; 6.12%)

Assess leisure activity by having the patients share their leisure experiences. Ask each patient to bring a song to the next group meeting which describes their leisure activity, hobby, or interests. 20

Encourage the patient to volunteer to assist in providing programming and running the hospital radio station. To develop music involvement, ask the patient to volunteer for "available positions in music" which are needed for music programming. 31

Involve the patient in musical games such as "Music Concentration." 30

IS-6   Does not listen/uninterested in listening to the desires and needs of others; interrupts peers when they are speaking or performing; does not respect the opinions of others (n1 = 2; 4.08%)

During music listening assign each group member a time to play their preferred music for the rest of the group. Make listening to and respecting each group member's right to play their music contingent upon getting a time to play one's own preferred music for the group (i.e. the patient who does not listen or participate appropriately loses his/her turn). 45

＊   ＊   ＊   ＊

Have the students work together to create a music video (including taping and editing) with original script/lyrics and musical accompaniment. 40

IS-7   Excessive fear of rejection; rejects others to avoid being rejected; excessive fear of not being accepted by others (n1 = 1; 2.04%)

Use round robin story telling. In the presence of background program music, give each patient three minutes to tell a story based on the music. After three minutes, ask a second patient to continue the story where the first patient left off. Each patient's participation is vital to the success of the activity. 43

IS-8   Uses inappropriate behavior as a means to gain attention (n1 = 1; 2.04%)

Reinforce patients who display appropriate behavior during the music therapy session (e.g., give first choice of instrument). 43

IS-9 Does not share or take turns (n1 = 1; 2.04%)

Involve the client in the playing of games in which the winner gets first chance, second chance, or third chance. 45

IS-10 Poor leadership skills; does not take the initiative (n1 = 1; 2.04%)

During an instrumental or vocal call and response activity give each student a chance to be the leader. 40

DRUGS (n = 12; 7.69%)

Includes:

D-1.0 SUBSTANCE USE OR ABUSE

D-2.0 MEDICATIONS (no problems submitted)

D-3.0 PHYSICAL WELL BEING (no problems submitted)

<u>PROBLEM</u>   <u>MUSIC THERAPY INTERVENTION</u>

D-1.1 Lacks knowledge of the effects of chemicals upon physical and psychological functioning; unaware of or denies chemical dependency or loss of self control (n1 = 4; 33.33%)

Discuss and interpret the lyrics of songs such as "Life In The Fast Lane" and "I'm Your Pusher." Encourage the patients to share their feelings/experiences during the discussion. Role play negative behaviors and consequences to increase self awareness. 20-46

Have the patients write about their abuse, getting their ideas from a list of song titles selected by the therapist and based upon the music preferences of the patients. 20

* * * *

Ask the patient to identify physical/psychological cravings present (elicited) when listening to music they formerly associated with the use of chemicals (e.g., "heavy metal" rock music). 50

D-1.2 Uses substances regularly; may be a maladaptive coping mechanism for stress or unpleasant situations; may use drugs for recreation (n1 = 3; 25.00%)

CTD (Clinical Training Director) note: Adolescents at this facility do not necessarily use the 12-step program. I have found a performance type of group to be more beneficial for our adolescents than a verbal/insight oriented group. 46

Replace recreational substance abuse with individual instrumental lessons. 43

* * * *

Teach relaxation techniques as a type of chemical-free stress management. 50

D-1.3 Uses substances to "control" behavior and to block feelings (to numb affect) (n1 = 2; 16.67%)

Use lyric analysis and discussion to assist the client in identifying and expressing feelings without drug use. 40

* * * *

Have the client identify feeling in music using an adjective checklist. 31

D-1.4 Experiences severe depression while mourning the loss of the substance (n1 = 1; 8.33%)

Utilize song writing to assist the patient in getting in touch with rehabilitation goals and in mourning the loss. 31

D-1.5 Client links own identity to substance abuse (i.e., "being a druggie") (n1 = 1; 8.33%)

Explore personal identity as it relates to music preferences, including the interrelation of music and substance abuse (i.e., lyrics which discuss drug use). 40

D-1.6 Lack of diaphragmatic control (from excessive purging associated with eating disorder) (n1 = 1; 8.33%)

During choir or individual voice lessons, use vocal exercises that focus on appropriate use of the diaphragm. 31

CODE: N = Number of music therapy interventions submitted for Adolescents.

n = Number of music therapy interventions submitted for the particular area of assessment. % = Percentage of N.

n1 = Number of music therapy interventions submitted for each component problem. % = Percentage of n1.

* * * * = Separates different types of music therapy interventions (e.g., playing instruments; singing; composing; moving to music; specified behavior modification techniques; other).

Number(s) after each intervention (e.g., 36) refers to the mean *GAF* score of the clients for whom the intervention was designed. One score was given by each music therapist specifying the intervention (e.g., "25-30-36" indicates that the particular intervention was submitted by three music therapists, and that the intervention was used with clients having the above mean *GAF* scores.

PSYCHIATRIC ASSESSMENTS AND TREATMENTS EMPLOYED IN NAMT-APPROVED CLINICAL TRAINING FACILITIES: CHILDREN (N = 122)

ASSESSMENT AREA

BEHAVIOR (n = 18; 14.75%)

PROBLEM   MUSIC THERAPY INTERVENTION

B-1 Unassertive; Does not express own needs; lacks inquiry skills (observe for anxiety or fears, evasiveness, or preoccupations); unable to express true feelings or opinions independent of peer pressure; feels compelled to agree with "the right" answer, or the answer given by peers ($n1$ = 6; 33.33%)

Ask the student to use pictures or signs to indicate choice of instrument to use during music activity. 20

Ask the student to conduct the group. Give the student a conductor's baton, and the group members a variety of instruments. Ask the student conducting to communicate dynamics, tempo and when the music should start or stop. 36

After playing a song in a small ensemble, ask the patient to talk about what she experienced while playing. 46

* * * *

Encourage the patient to actively participate by expressing own spontaneous feelings and opinions when prompted during song discussion. 3 6

* * * *

When discussing problem solving or conflict situations, each patient will take turns stating opinions which agree and differ from those stated by the majority of patients. 36

* * * *

Play musical games which require the client to ask questions. 36

B-2   Attention deficit; lack of attention span; distracted by internal/external
stimuli; does not maintain interest in task; poor concentration skills ($n1 = 5$;
27.78%)

During singing activities, encourage the child to finish singing the song
while maintaining a rhythmic beat. 56

Given the lyrics of a song, ask the staff or a student to read the lyrics.
Observe whether each student remains seated, listens quietly, and talks
appropriately (i.e., only when asked). 50

*   *   *   *

Reinforce in seat behavior using instrument play activities. 36

*   *   *   *

Require that the patient complete the assigned task before moving on to
another task/comment. 36

Arrange the musical task to provide incentive for focus of attention and
completion. 45

B-3   Does not take turns (e.g., impulsively grabs instrument) ($n1 = 3$; 16.67%)

Write a list of 11 roles coveted by the children (e.g., leading the group in
the playing of instruments). Assign a number (2 through 12) to each
role, so that when two die are rolled, the number appearing on the die is
also the number of a role. Each child then takes turns rolling the die and
assuming the role. 40

Involve the client in a rhythm band in which each person changes
instruments upon cue. 56

*   *   *   *

Utilize a song which requires everyone to take turns. Encourage the
client to take turns communicating to the group. 36

B-4   Hits peers ($n1 = 3$; 16.67%)

Involve the client in a puppet show focused on a musical drama about
feelings. 56

*   *   *   *

Encourage appropriate use of rhythm sticks (i.e., doesn't hit peers). 50

* * * *

Make participation in coveted music therapy activity contingent upon keeping hands, feet, and objects to self. 40

B-5	Exhibits poor eye contact (n_1 = 1; 5.56%)

Sing the child's name in a song. The therapist presents own hands before the child and offers to do a push and pull activity. 45

AFFECT (n = 10; 8.20%)

<u>PROBLEM</u>   <u>MUSIC THERAPY INTERVENTION</u>

A-1   Impaired ability to Identify/expresses feelings; demonstrates affect inappropriate to mood; facial expression may be flat, blunt, labile, or sad; poor vocabulary of feeling words (n_1 = 10; 100.00%)

Give the patient a set of cards, each card having the drawing of a person's face depicting a specific emotion (e.g., happy; sad; mad). Ask the patient to identify the feeling depicted, and how the feeling is frequently expressed. Have the patient then select an instrument and nonverbally express the same feeling using the instrument, or select a song that correlates with the emotion. (Note: A variation of this activity is to first, have the patients draw facial features that express basic emotions, then follow-up with the above music activities). 33-40

Give instruments to the group then ask the group to play a specific feeling (e.g., the therapist says "Lets sound sad." The children then play how they think sad should sound.). Follow-up with a discussion of what makes each child feel sad. 36

Ask the patients to express specific feelings by playing rhythm instruments. Observe for appropriate feeling response. 86

* * * *

Have the group sing the song, "If You're Happy and You Know It" while moving as if they are happy. Vary the activity to elicit different emotions by changing the lyrics (e.g., "If you're sad and you know it...") and the accompanying movements. 40

Sing the peekaboo song using a soft scarf to hide the therapist's face from the client. At the end of the song pull the scarf away and say "boo!" Note the quality of the client's affective response. 45

* * * *

Have the clients listen to short musical selections, then indicate through facial expressions how they felt while listening. Vary the activity by having clients report verbally how they felt while listening. 50

Have the patient listen to a variety of musical styles. Include music which the patient both prefers and does not prefer. Ask the patient to discuss her preferences. 46

* * * *

Play the game, "Music Bingo" to nonverbal music. 56

Observe whether the student shows appropriate affective response (e.g., laughter; humor; smiling; anticipation) during music activities. 20

SENSORY (n = 6; 4.92%)

PROBLEM	MUSIC THERAPY INTERVENTION

S-1   Lacks auditory sequential memory (listening; auditory perception) ($n1 = 3$; 50.00%)

Assess the patient's ability to follow sequential steps given aurally. Given instruction on how to play rhythm instruments, present the client with various types and numbers of rhythm instruments. Play the instruments in sequential order and ask the client to repeat the sequence (e.g., First strike the drum, then the cymbal, and then the resonator bell. Ask the client to imitate) 36

* * * *

Conduct music activities in which children must listen to, then follow directions. 50

* * * *

Have the client listen to age-appropriate music, then tell about the musical characteristics, such as form and instrumentation. 40

S-2	Lacks auditory discrimination skills (listening; auditory perception)
(n_1 = 3; 50.00%)	

First assess the ability to discriminate gross musical sounds (e.g., discriminates the sound of a drum from a piano). Next assess the ability to make finer auditory discriminations, such as speech sounds (e.g., discriminates male from female voice; discriminates words and syllables) and more subtle music sounds. 36

Have the client listen to age-appropriate music, then tell about the musical characteristics, such as form and instrumentation. 40

Utilize music listening activities to teach concepts such as start and stop, loud and quiet, and fast and slow. Have students match the concept with the type of music heard (e.g., Client says "fast" when fast music is played and "slow" when slow music is played. Also, have students identify concepts using alternative communication techniques (i.e., signs; picture symbol cards). 20

IMAGERY (n = 2; 1.64%)

PROBLEM   MUSIC THERAPY INTERVENTION

IM-1 Inability to experience thoughts when attempting to relax (n_1 = 1;
50.00%)

Have the client listen to quiet, relaxing music without talking, then give verbal feedback about their experience. 50

IM-2 Inability to use imagination to develop stories (n_1 = 1; 50.00%)

Have the clients listen to quiet music as they draw/express themselves on paper. 50

COGNITIVE (n = 18; 14.75%)

<u>PROBLEM</u>   <u>MUSIC THERAPY INTERVENTION</u>

C-1   Difficulty following directions; consider the difficulty of the instructions, the physical ability to follow directions, retention ability, and the ability to accept or listen to instructions (n1 = 6; 33.33%)

Involve the client in instrumental tasks, such as learning a pattern on a xylophone, or a rhythmic pattern on the drum. 46

Have the patients develop a code language, communicated with rhythm instruments. After the code is developed, divide the patients into two groups, then let each group take turns sending messages (directives) to the other group. When a group receives a directive, they must follow the directive by performing the task requested in the directive. 40

* * * *

During group singing, require the client to listen for page numbers to be announced, then turn to the correct page. 33

During group singing, ask the client to find the page number of a song by looking in the table of contents. Also, given commands such as "Look in the back of the book;" "Look in the front of the book;" "Look at the top of the page;" "Look at the bottom of the page." 33

* * * *

Present songs containing one-step, two-step, and multi-step directions (e.g., body action songs such as "clap your hands, pat your knees, then stomp your feet" to the tune, "If You're Happy and You Know It;" movement to music; circle or other simple dances). 45

* * * *

Make raising one's hand before speaking contingent upon choice of music instrument or song. 40

C-2   Lacks directionality and spatial concepts (n1 = 3; 16.67%)

Use music activities designed to teach concepts such as right from left, and up from down (See: W. Janiak (1978). *Songs for Music Therapy*). 36

Observe spatial awareness in relation to objects in the room by having the student to walk around the outer perimeter of a circle of chairs during a music activity. 20

Observe spatial awareness in relation to other students by asking the student to line up next to/behind/in front of another student for music movement activities. 20

C-3 Low self-esteem; negative self concept; makes negative self-statements; may refuse to participate in group activities (n1 = 2; 11.11%)

When assessing the success of music accomplishments, record the number of positive self statements and positive peer statements which are made independent of prompts. 36

* * * *

Play the game, "Music Charades" in which clients take turns creatively moving to nonverbal music, as the other clients try to guess the feeling being expressed. The goal is increased self-confidence through successful group participation. 56

C-4 Observe method and quality of approach to tasks (e.g., disorganized vs. goal directed; fast without concern for quality vs. slow and deliberate; gives up easily vs. perseverance; inaccurate vs. accurate) (n1 = 1; 5.56%)

Teach the patient to perform a song on an instrument, such as using the autoharp to provide a chordal accompaniment, or playing an ostinato pattern on the marimba. 46

C-5 Manipulates using intimidation (makes derogatory comments to peers to effect specific behavior) (n1 = 1; 5.56%)

During song writing, teach the sharing of concepts by singing the children's thoughts, feelings, and ideas about appropriate ways of meeting one's needs. 56

C-6 Lacks temporal or time concepts (n1 = 1; 5.56%)

Use music activities designed to teach time skills (See: C. L. Reichard & Dennis B. Blackburn (1973). *Music Based Instruction for the Exceptional Child*). 36

| C-7 | Lacks money concepts ($n1 = 1$; 5.56%) |

Use music activities designed to teach money concepts (See: C. L. Reichard & Dennis B. Blackburn (1973). *Music Based Instruction for the Exceptional Child*). 36

| C-8 | Recalls letters of the alphabet ($n1 = 1$; 5.56%) |

Play games such as "Musical Anagrams" (see the *Music Therapy Source Book*). Fill in blanks on the blackboard to spell the name of a favorite singer or instrument. Sing a song about the letters of the alphabet (e.g., "The Alphabet Song"), stopping the song at various points and asking a client to point to the letter being sung. 33

| C-9 | Poor counting skills; may not remember correct numerical sequence ($n1 = 1$; 5.56%) |

Ask the client to find a specific page number in a songbook. 33

| C-10 | Poor reading and writing skills ($n1 = 1$; 5.56%) |

Assign the student to use the school library to compile a music notebook about music of other lands. 40

INTERPERSONAL-SOCIALIZATION ($n = 32$; 26.23%)

PROBLEM   MUSIC THERAPY INTERVENTION

| IS-1 | Exhibits disruptive or socially inappropriate behavior; may exhibit disruptive outbursts to attract attention; breaks rules; may make negative comments to peers resulting in rejection by peers; does not make constructive suggestions ($n1 = 9$; 28.13%) |

Make music therapy activities such as singing, listening, moving, creating music, and playing instruments contingent upon classroom discipline. Utilize a point system (Various methods are used: (1) Write each student's name on a large poster and tack the poster to the wall. Next to each name place five plastic push pins, each representing a certain number of minutes the student may spend in a music activity. Pull a pin for each occurrence of inappropriate behavior (response cost). (2) Same as "1" except give pins for appropriate behavior and pull pins for inappropriate behavior. (3) Have the student carry a chart; the chart must be initialed by all or a predetermined number of the student's teachers, verifying good classroom behavior, in order to participate in music activities). 40

During general music therapy activities, if a student fails to demonstrate desired behavior, initiate a step-wise discipline procedure beginning with a "stop and think" verbal reminder, followed by removal from the activity, then from the group if the behavior does not comply. 40

Make each child being the conductor for her favorite song contingent upon appropriate behavior. 56

Make good grades in music contingent upon appropriate participation in music activities. Give check marks for positive behavior. 50

* * * *

During song lyric discussion involving staff and clients, reinforce constructive criticism, suggestions, and interpretations about the content of the song lyrics. 50

* * * *

Ask the patients to remain quiet while listening to a selection of music. Observe responses. 86

* * * *

Involve the student in as many group music activities as possible, particularly those requiring interpersonal interaction. 36

* * * *

Ask the patients to assist in putting together a musical collage of a group of musical artists. Observe for disruptive behavior. 86

* * * *

Involve the client in creative marching to upbeat nonverbal music. 56

IS-2 Withdraws; minimal or no verbal interaction; does not participate in group activities; avoids interaction with peers; shy; timid; not interested in peers (n_1 = 8; 25.00%)

Use a music rhythm band to encourage nonverbal interaction. 56

Have the patient repeat a rhythmic pattern on the claves. Increase the difficulty of the rhythm. Switch roles; have the patient initiate the rhythm pattern and the therapist imitate. 46

Have the student initiate appropriate verbal interaction with another student during routine interactive music activities (e.g., "Do you want the drum?" "Will you be my partner?" "Hold the autoharp while I strum."). 20

*   *   *   *

Ask each patient to bring a song to the music therapy session that describes their relationship with a peer. Ask each patient to play the song, then discuss their relationship with the peer. 86

Ask the client to choose a song that a peer would enjoy. 33

*   *   *   *

Involve the client in as many group music activities as possible. 20-36

*   *   *   *

Encourage the patient to interact positively with peers during a greeting song activity. 36

IS-3 Uncooperative with adults and peers; argues with peers; does not negotiate or compromise (n1 = 7; 21.88%)

Have the patient repeat a rhythmic pattern on the claves. Increase the difficulty of the rhythm. Switch roles; have the patient initiate the rhythm pattern and the therapist imitate. Note quality of interaction (e.g., fearful; comfortable; domineering; defensive) with adults/authority figures. 46

Involve the client in ensemble tasks such as Orff instrumental activities. Observe for appropriate peer interactions (e.g., mutuality in interactions; problem solving). 46

Play the "Musical Search Game:" (1) Let instrumental sounds represent movement cues (e.g., The sound of the tambourine means to walk forward; the sound of the maracas means to turn; a loud drum beat means the searcher is getting closer to the hidden object; a soft drum beat means the searcher is going away from the hidden object; the sound of a high pitched rhythm instrument (triangle, high pitched tone or xylophone bar) means to reach up; the sound of a low pitched rhythm instrument (low pitched tone or xylophone bar or bass drum) means to reach down. (2) Choose a client to be the searcher, blindfold the searcher, and tell the searcher that her peers will provide "hints" (cues) for finding the hidden object by playing the rhythm instruments. An adult or another peer may act as "Sound Department Director," specifying when each instrument is to be played (NOTE: This role may be eliminated as students gain experience with the game). 36

Have the patients assist one another with the construction of music instruments. Observe social behavior. 86

* * * *

Divide the patients into groups of three or four. Give each group a stack of recordings and ask them to select three songs they would like to hear. 86

Have the client work with a peer in choosing a song that suits both of them. 33

* * * *

Involve the student in a music activity which requires cooperation/ teamwork with a peer. Observe whether the student responds appropriately to other students' nonverbal and verbal socialization efforts. 20

| IS-4   Does not share ($n1$ = 4; 12.50%) |

Ask the client to equally divide the time that she and her peers get to play an instrument. 50

Give two clients a set of bongos or a large drum and ask them to play the drum together while following the directives of the song (e.g., "Play the drum soft;" "Play the drum loud"); have the children share other rhythm instruments. 45-50

* * * *

Involve the children in the playing of musical games in which they must share or take turns. 50

| IS-5   Interrupts the speaker and activity by extraneous talking ($n1$ = 1; 3.13%) |

Reinforce on task behavior through active participation in a pentatonic ensemble. Use eye contact to communicate when each individual is to start and stop playing her instrument. 36

| IS-6   Inaudible speaking voice ($n1$ = 1; 3.13%) |

During group singing, ask the client to announce, loud enough for the group to hear, a song choice to the group. 33

IS-7   Lacks leadership skills (n1 = 1; 3.13%)

Give the child experience at assuming and maintaining a leadership role during rhythm instrument activities. Give the child "stop" and "go" signs, asking her to signal the group when to start playing and when to stop playing their instruments. 45

IS-8   Does not express or respond to greetings or closings (i.e., good-byes) (n1 = 1; 3.13%)

Use a greeting song (e.g., "Hello Song") at the beginning of the session and a good-bye song (e.g., Good-bye client's name to the tune of "Good Night Ladies") at the end of the session. Prompt verbal hellos and good-byes using appropriate gestures (e.g., hand shaking) (See: Konnie K. Saliba, *Good Morning Songs & Wake-Up Games*). 45

DRUGS (n = 18; 14.75%)

Includes:

D-1.0 PHYSICAL WELL BEING

D-2.0 PHYSICAL COMMUNICATION PROBLEMS

D-3.0 SUBSTANCE ABUSE and MEDICATIONS (No problems submitted)

<u>PROBLEM</u>   <u>MUSIC THERAPY INTERVENTION</u>

D-1.1 Impaired gross motor coordination; difficulty performing basic movement tasks; awkward when attempting common movements such as walking; runs into people when in a group (n1 = 5; 28.78%)

Involve the client in music movement activities which incorporate skills such as walking, skipping, hopping, and marching. Model the movements using songs which specify the type of movement in the lyrics (e.g., W. Janiak, *Songs for Music Therapy*, "Hop Like a Bunny"). 46

During creative movement to music, have the client mirror movements and lead movements for peers. 36

Involve the client in music activities such as mirroring movements, imitating object/animal movement (e.g., The clients walk like a turkey after doing the Thanksgiving turkey chant [C. Bitcon, *Alike and*

Different]), moving to various tempi, and working with a partner or the group in movement tasks. 40

Involve the children in musical games involving gross motor movements. 50

Beat a mano drum while the clients walk to the beat. Ask the clients to adjust their walking pace when the beat is varied. Play the drum in different positions (i.e., right side up; up side down; sideways), letting each position represent a different way to walk (i.e., forward; backward; sideways). 36

D-1.2 Lacks finger dexterity (fine motor) ($n1 = 2$; 11.11%)

Give individual keyboard instruction emphasizing melodies and finger exercises utilizing all five fingers. Encourage independent finger movement. 36-51

D-1.3 Has difficulty grasping or manipulating utensils; does not utilize fine motor skills commensurate with age level; impaired grasp function (e.g., palmer; pincer ($n1 = 2$; 11.11%)

Involve the client in instrumental music activities (e.g., pushing buttons to play the autoharp; grasping a guitar/autoharp pick; playing the finger cymbals; finger strums on the guitar; using mallets to play tone bars). 45-46

D-1.4 Lacks eye-hand motor coordination ($n1 = 2$; 11.11%)

Have the clients listen to a recorded performance of "Bell Dance." Replay the recording and ask the clients to play along using resonator bells. 50

* * * *

Ask the clients to listen to a recording of "To the Music I." Replay the recording and ask the clients to clap when the command to clap is given in the lyrics (claps on cue). Note correct/incorrect clapping. 50

D-1.5 Often drops objects causing disruptions to others and embarrassment to self ($n1 = 1$; 5.55%)

Involve the client in instrumental activities. Encourage the client to hold the instrument. 40

D-2.1 Cannot describe objects, feelings, or situations; lacks descriptive skills; note whether verbal quality is logical, coherent, and concrete vs. abstract, and whether language development is appropriate for age (n1 = 2; 11.11%)

Ask the patient to listen to the "words" of a song and then tell what took place in the song. 46

* * * *

Tell or give the patient several objects, feelings, or situations and ask the patient to describe them without mentioning the name of the object, feeling, or situation. Encourage the patient's search for descriptive qualities; play "detective" games. 36

D-2.2 Impaired ability to Imitate speech or nonspeech sounds (n1 = 1; 5.55%)

Use songs such as "Old Mac Donald" and "The Wheels on the Bus" to elicit the imitation of animal sounds, sounds of environmental objects (i.e., the bus), and speech sounds (song lyrics). 45

D-2.3 Exhibits explosive rather than a comfortable level of speech (n1 = 1; 5.55%)

Engage the client in group singing, giving each member a solo. 56

D-2.4 Poor speech articulation (n1 = 1; 5.55%)

Engage the client in the singing of songs; chant the lyrics; emphasize clear pronunciation. 40

D-2.5 Impaired receptive language ability; poor comprehension (n1 = 1; 5.55%)

Discuss the meaning of song lyrics; critique musical performances. 40

CODE: N = Number of music therapy interventions submitted for Children.

n = Number of music therapy interventions submitted for the particular area of assessment. % = Percentage of N.

n1 = Number of music therapy interventions submitted for each component problem. % = Percentage of n1.

* * * * = Separates different types of music therapy interventions
(e.g., playing instruments; singing; composing; moving to music;
specified behavior modification techniques; other).

Number(s) after each intervention (e.g., 36) refers to the mean *GAF*
score of the clients for whom the intervention is designed. One score was
given by each music therapist specifying the intervention (e.g., "25-30-
36" indicates that the particular intervention was submitted by three
music therapists, and that the intervention is used with clients having the
above mean *GAF* scores).

PSYCHIATRIC MUSIC THERAPY ASSESSMENTS AND TREATMENTS EMPLOYED IN NAMT-APPROVED CLINICAL TRAINING FACILITIES
ADULTS: MUSIC BEHAVIOR

(Combined, N = 364; Male, $N1$ = 147; 40.39% Female, $N2$ = 217; 59.62%)

ASSESSMENT AREA

LISTENING TO MUSIC (Combined, n = 112; 30.77%; Male, $n1$ = 47; 41.96%; Female, $n5$ = 65; 58.04%)

BEHAVIOR   MUSIC THERAPY INTERVENTION

L-1	Demonstrates musical preferences ($n3$ = 12; $n4$ = 24; $n5$ = 36; 32.14%)

When asked, the client will express preference for a favorite music style, performer, or composer. NOTE: The therapist may wish to follow-up by playing the preferred song for the client and inviting the client to join in the singing of the lyrics. M-25-30-30-32; F-26-30-31-35-36-39-50-65

Given a collection of recordings or albums, the patient will select a song to play for the group (e.g., Given a table with a stack of twenty albums, ask the client to go to the table and pick an album to play for the group; an alternative is to ask the patient to bring a recording from her personal record collection, or to select a recording from the record library in the music therapy room). Follow-up with lyric interpretation and discussion. THERAPIST NOTE: If the patient does not respond to this procedure in a group situation, repeat the procedure in an individualized or one-to-one session with the patient. Songs used should have recovery themes. F-25-30-31-39-60

Involve the client in a discussion of musical preferences. Assign the client to research the topic of music in the hospital library, then share the resulting information with the group. Assign the client to listen to the music of a particular composer, to gather historical information about the composer, and then to present to the group an oral report (with recorded musical examples) about the style of the composer. M-35; F-41-37

Ask the patient to identify music-related activities he or she engages in at home (e.g., listening to records; watching musicals on television; listening to music on the radio; visiting music stores; going to concerts and recitals). M-40; F-35

Ask the client to bring recordings of and information about one of their preferred musical artists to present to the group. M-85; F-31

During music listening, ask the patients to rate their preference for the songs played. Give each patient the opportunity to share their music ratings with others (e.g., Play "Rate a Record" in which various musical selections are played and each patient rates their preference for each selection using a 10-point scale). M-30; F-65

Show the patient the catalogued collection of recordings and ask him to choose a recording of his favorite artist for music listening. Encourage the patient to talk about his favorite recordings or albums. M-40

Make a music preferences tape in which many styles of music are represented. Play the tape and ask the client to say "yes" or "no" to indicate her preference for each style of music. F-25

Ask the group to rank given musical compositions in the order they are to be played. Encourage group discussion of the aspects of each composition (e.g., positive aspects versus negative aspects). M-35

Administer a questionnaire that requires the patient to identify the type of music she listens to when she is happy, the type she listens to when she is sad, and what she likes best about the music (e.g., may include comments about the lyrics, melody, beat, or tempo). F-56

Given a list of 30 songs, the patient will select one song for the group to sing. M-35

Have each patient select a song to play for the group. After the group has listened attentively to each song, discuss the song. Have the group rank in order the songs from most preferred to least preferred. F-37

Initiate music listening independently during the session and/or leisure time. M-30

Include questions on the assessment questionnaire to identify the patient's preferred modality (e.g., art; music; dance; movement; recreation) for addressing treatment issues. F-56

The patient identifies her preferred music by selecting music to be played, and then states why she prefers the music. F-32

Assess the client's music preferences by asking the client to sing a cappella a song of her choice. Follow-up by playing on the piano the song that the client sang, in the key in which it was sung. F-26

> **L-2**   Demonstrates familiarity with and enjoyment of a variety of styles of music; respects the musical preferences of others; listens attentively to song and lyrics; focuses on the meaning of lyrics ($n3 = 8$; $n4 = 8$; $n5 = 16$; 14.29%)

After playing a song lasting # minutes, have the patient state what the song is about, how it relates to herself, the style of music, and whether or not she likes the song. M-30; M-51; F-30-32-35-51

Ask the client to listen to a song then select one line related to current issues. M-41; F-41

Encourage each client to listen to, and to make supportive statements regarding the musical preferences of other group members. M-26; F-26

Observe whether the client participates in lyric analysis. M-40

Ask the client to bring a song to the music therapy session that describes a topic of interest. M-85

Given a style of music, have the client choose a song representative of the style. M-75

Observe the client's willingness to listen to different styles of music and to participate in group discussions about contrasting styles. F-41

Have a group discussion in which each client tells the group his favorite songs and performers, then plays a recording of the song for the group. M-31

Observe whether the client refrains from speaking while listening to music. F-25

> **L-3**   Shares personal knowledge or recollections associated with musical preferences; contributes to group discussions about music; demonstrates the ability to recognize and relate specific musical qualities or characteristics to personal preferences and significant life memories; relates abstract concepts in music to one's own experience ($n3 = 6$; $n4 = 3$; $n5 = 9$; 8.04%)

Ask the client to listen to a song and, based upon the client's familiarity with the song, share information, ideas, or memories relating to the song lyrics or music. M-41-30; F-41

Ask the patient to request or identify some favorite songs. After listening to each song, ask the patient to explain the song's qualities and the particular personal significance of the song. M-40

Ask the patient to listen to a song while thinking of memories, ideas, hopes, wishes, and feelings, he would like to keep. Draw a picture of a bottle and ask the patient to imagine the bottle signifies himself. Tell the patient you are going to play the song, "Time in a Bottle." Ask the patient to list, while the song is playing, memories or things he would like to keep inside the bottle. Also, the patient should list, or put outside the bottle, things he would like to forget, or get rid of. M-35

During lyric analysis, observe whether the client is able to relate personal issues (e.g., his home life) to the song lyrics. After listening to the song, prompt the client to discuss his family life and his future goals. M-31

Present the client with a variety of songs. Ask the client to pick out one song that best describes herself, her day, and her future. Next, ask the client to tell how or why the song describes herself, her day, and her future. F-20

Ask the client to choose a song that describes her feelings and then to play the song for the group. F-26

Play a recording of a well-known performer and ask the group if they know anything about the performer or the song. Observe which clients contribute to the group discussion about the performer or the song. M-40

L-4   Chooses music to promote own relaxation; enjoys easy listening music (n3 = 1; n4 = 5; n5 = 6; 5.36%)

Assess the patient's ability to use music listening to promote relaxation. Ask the patient to choose music for relaxation. Does the patient have sufficient attention span to participate in relaxation to music? Test the patient's ability to attend to a task for increasing periods of time (e.g., 10 minutes, then 15 minutes, etc.). M-30; F-30-60

Play ten relaxing music selections for the client. Ask the client to rate each selection in terms of how relaxing she perceives the music to be. F-35

Assess/develop the client's ability to use both vocal and instrumental music to promote relaxation exercises. Have the client do muscle relaxation exercises (tensing followed relaxation of specific muscle groups) to instrumental music, and deep breathing to produce vocal tones. F-35

Play easy listening music and ask the patient to listen and describe any images that come to mind. F-30

L-5   Selects preferred music that expresses present or past feelings (n3 = 3; n4 = 2; n5 = 5; 4.46%)

Present the client with numerous recordings representing a variety of styles of music. Ask the client to select a musical preference that

expresses how he or she is feeling today or has felt in the past.
M-41-26;   F-41

Given a list of 300 songs, ask the patient to choose a song that describes how she
feels, or which describes an issue she is presently working on.
Encourage the patient to not choose her favorite song. F-56

After playing the music have patients talk about feelings they associate with
the music. M-35

L-6   Demonstrates musical awareness when listening; exhibits discriminatory
listening skills ($n3 = 3$; $n4 = 1$; $n5 = 4$; 3.57%)

Ask the client to complete a music listening questionnaire while listening
to the music. Questions on the questionnaire should be focused toward
assessing the client's degree of musical awareness, and be arranged in
order of difficulty from easy to difficult. Such questions, for example,
might require the client to identify the music played (e.g., composer,
title, artist), identify the category or style of music, identify the
instruments heard and any changing tempos, identify feelings elicited
by the music, and rate the music on a scale of 1 to 10, with 1 being most
preferred. Clients may be asked to give an explanation of their rating.
M-75;   F-30

Play a variety of styles of music and ask the patients to identify the style
being played. M-35

Teach the patients to hear chord changes while listening to recorded
music. M-30

L-7   Demonstrates the ability to associate affect with corresponding music; verbalizes
perceived mood of preferred music; identifies the mood of the music ($n3 = 1$; $n4 = 3$;
$n5 = 4$; 3.57%)

The patient listens to preferred music she has previously selected and
verbalizes her perceptions of the mood of the music. F-32

Give the patient two musical selections with an explanation of the nature of the
pieces if they are unfamiliar. After listening to the selections ask the patient to
express his opinion of the selections. M-40

Play unfamiliar instrumental music compositions that have
descriptive song titles (e.g., "Listen to the Wind," "Dance of the Windup
Toy," "Rain"). Have the patients guess the song title, or to make up a title
to the music. F-32

Play "The Erlking" (Schubert, 1815). Ask patients to identify feelings
they perceive in the music. NOTE: "The Erlking" ("Der Erlkonig") is a
song about "...the tragic ride of a father trying to out distance the Erlking,
Death. The three characters of Goethe's poem are portrayed in the voice

part: the child who sees Death, the father who tries to give him courage, and the enticing voice of the Erlking. Suggesting rapid hoof beats and a pounding pulse, the piano accompaniment keeps an exciting rhythm going throughout. Only at the end, on a dark chord – the Neapolitan sixth, ...does the motion stop. The singer gasps the final line, 'In his arms the child was dead,' and the song is over (Lloyd, 1968, p. 513)." F-30

L-8   Recognizes or recalls the titles of well-known, age-appropriate songs when they are played ($n3 = 0$; $n4 = 3$; $n5 = 3$; 2.68%)

Conduct the "Name That Tune" activity to assist clients in identifying the melody of familiar songs. Use songs that have been played in previous music therapy sessions. The songs presented should have recovery themes. If clients have difficulty identifying the name of the song, provide cues or prompts (e.g., Play the song, "The Rose." If the clients do not respond ask them to name some songs with the word "rose" in the title). F-60; F-30

Conduct a "Name That Tune" activity. Play songs and ask patients to name their titles. F-25

L-9   Chooses a song for group listening ($n3 = 2$; $n4 = 1$; $n5 = 3$; 2.68%)

The client is give a list of 100 songs from which to choose. If the client's favorite song is not on the list, ask the client to name a song to add to the list. After singing the song the therapists may wish to involve the clients in a discussion of the lyrics. M-40; F-50

If the client enjoys playing recordings for the group, arrange for the client to serve as the disc jockey at the next patient party. M-25

L-10 Distinguishes and identifies characteristics of music (e.g., dynamics; tempo; timbre) ($n3 = 2$; $n4 = 1$; $n5 = 3$; 2.68%)

Have the patient match the changes in the music by playing a rhythm instrument (e.g., plays loud to loud music; slow to slow music). M-30; F-30

Assess the patient's ability to distinguish between instruments of different timbre. Ask the patient to close his eyes. Play two different instrumental timbres (e.g., the drum followed by a resonator bell). Ask the patient to identify whether the timbres were the same or different. Next ask the patient to identify the name of the instruments played and the order in which they were played. M-25

L-11 Listens to music but does not identify musical preferences; may fear peers will not like choice of music (n3 = 1; n4 = 2; n5 = 3; 2.68%)

Play various styles of music and ask the patient to listen to the music and rate his or her preference for it. M-51; F-51

Ask the client to play her favorite recording, then to ask her peers what the song makes them think of. F-20

L-12 Chooses music that describes self (n3 = 1; n4 = 2; n5 = 3; 2.68%)

Give the patient numerous recordings and ask him to choose a song that describes himself. M-35

Ask the patient to introduce herself to the group by picking a song that best describes herself. F-60

Given her preferred song, ask the client to choose a sentence from the song that best describes herself. F-39

L-13 Identifies the names of musical instruments used in a recording (n3 = 2; n4 = 0; n5 = 2; 1.79%)

Ask the client to listening to a recording and to identify the names of any music instruments recognized. M-32

Play a music recording in which the sounds of specific instruments can be heard. Associate the sound of an instrument with the actual instrument, or a picture of the instrument. Follow-up by fading out visual aids so the client can identify the instrument from an aural presentation. M-31

L-14 Demonstrates the ability to perceive music (n3 = 1; n4 = 1; n5 = 2; 1.79%)

Ask the client to demonstrate an observable response to the music as it is playing (i.e., facial; movement). M-30

During music listening, observe any unprompted physical responses to the beat or rhythm. F-30

L-15 Sleeps when listening to music (apparently enjoys music listening as evidenced by regular attendance to the listening laboratory) (n3 = 1; n4 = 1; n5 = 2; 1.79%)

Provide the patient with colored pencils and paper. Ask the patient to draw his or her impressions while listening to the music. M-21; F-21

L-16 Patient listens to one recording repeatedly, in multiple succession to the exclusion of other recordings (n3 = 1; n4 = 1; n5 = 2; 1.79%)

Provide positive reinforcement (e.g., tokens, points, or edibles) for choosing to listen to different music. M-21; F-21

L-17 Demonstrates knowledge of relaxing music (n3 = 1; n4 = 1; n5 = 2; 1.79%)

The client is given a list of relaxing musical recordings and asked to choose her preferred recordings for future listening. M-51; F-51

L-18 Uses musical equipment independently (n3 = 0; n4 = 1; n5 = 1; 00.89%)

Ask the client to use a variety of music listening equipment (e.g., tape recorder; record player; video tape player; compact disc player) then observe her ability to use it. F-30

L-19 Listens to music independently (n3 = 0; n4 = 1; n5 = 1; 00.89%)

Observe whether the patient listens to music during her leisure time. F-30

L-20 Demonstrates the ability to locate sound sources (n3 = 1; n4 = 0; n5 = 1; 00.89%)

Ask the patient to close his eyes. The therapist turns on a sound source located in the room, then asks the patient to open his eyes and to point to where the music is coming from. M-25

L-21 Chooses music that describes a peer (n3 = 0; n4 = 1; n5 = 1; 00.89%)

During group listening, give a patient numerous recordings and ask her to choose a song that describes personal qualities of the peer on her left. F-60

L-22 Prefers specific elements of music (n3 = 0; n4 = 1; n5 = 1; 00.89%)

Play a preferred song for the patient. Ask the patient whether they prefer the lyrics, the melody, or the beat of the song best. F-31

L-23 Expresses likes as well as dislikes regarding a musical selection (n3 = 0; n4 = 1; n5 = 1; 00.89%)

Select a variety of songs representative of the style of music the patient prefers. Each song selected should be different from the others, in terms of tempo, volume, orchestration, and the theme of the lyrics. Play the songs and ask the patient to indicate their relative preference for the songs by rating the songs on a five point scale. After the patient finishes rating the songs, assist the patient in making decisions about what she specifically likes or dislikes about each song. Also, ask the patient to identify professional performing groups that sound similar to her preferred songs. F-31

L-24 Chooses appropriate background music ($n3 = 0$; $n4 = 1$; $n5 = 1$; 00.89%)

During a poetry writing session, assign a patient to choose appropriate background music to play during the recitation of the poem. The music should be appropriate to the mood and content of the poem. F-31

SINGING (Combined, $n = 75$; 20.60%; Male, $n1 = 28$; 37.33%; Female, $n2 = 47$; 62.67%)

BEHAVIOR   MUSIC THERAPY INTERVENTION

S-1   Participates in group sing-a-long; sings with group to piano or guitar accompaniment; indicates a desire to sing ($n3 = 7$; $n4 = 9$; $n5 = 16$; 21.33%)

Observe quality of participation (e.g., cooperates; takes turns requesting songs; sings in harmony with others; rhythm; vocal tone; pitch). M-30-25; F-37-30-65

Have the patients make decisions about which songs to sing during an informal sing-a-long. Given a list of 30 songs, have each patient select one song for the group to sing. M-25-35; F-26-32

Ask the patient to select a song from a song list for the group to sing, and then to sing the song with the group. M-32-30; F-35

Give patients the opportunity to sing Blues songs.

Ask the patient to name any song for the group to sing, such as their favorite or most memorable song. F-30

Encourage patients to talk about their favorite groups during the sing-a-long. Use the patients' preferred music in the sing-a-long. If a patient is experienced at playing piano, guitar, or drums, invite the patient to use their instrument to accompany the sing-a-long. M-25

Give the patient a music instrument and ask the patient to play the instrument while singing (order this task according to the ability level of the patient). F-41

Allot time for song dedication during the sing-a-long. Ask each client to select a song and dedicate it to a peer. The group then sings the song. F-60

S-2   Performs a vocal solo before the group; expresses a desire to perform a vocal solo, or to perform on stage; spontaneously sings a solo (n3 = 3; n4 = 9; n5 = 12; 16%)

Arrange for the patient to sing a solo before an audience (e.g., at the weekly talent show; ask the client to select, from a booklet of patriotic songs, a favorite song to sing at the Fourth of July unit picnic). F-25-30-35

The patient rehearses with the therapist a song of choice to sing for the group. M-25

Identify the name of the song the patient most often sings before her peers. Praise the patient for singing a solo. During the group sing-a-long, ask the patient to sing each verse solo and the group to join in on the chorus. An alternative is to have the patient sing each chorus solo and the group to join in on the verse. F-30

Ask the patient to choose a song, then to sing the song through a microphone during the weekly sing-a-long. F-35

During the talent show, ask the client to select any song (not limited to the song book) and to sing the song for the group using a microphone. F-35

Have the client to select a song, practice the song, then perform a vocal solo of the song before an audience (e.g., the Christmas pageant). F-30

The client will sing at least 50% of a song, with no prompts, in front of a group of familiar people. M-30

Arrange a room with stage lights and chairs. Have the client to give a recital in which he sings his favorite songs. M-31

Ask the client to pick a song that will "help her make it through the day." Arrange for the client to sing the song to the group to reinforce the positive benefit of the song lyrics, and to boost the client's self-esteem. F-30

Do a group rap that requires each patient to chant a solo line. F-65

S-3   Sings and follows a choral part (n3 = 3; n4 = 2; n5 = 5; 6.67%)

Demonstrate to the client how to sing and follow a choral part. Encourage the client to ask for assistance if needed. M-30; F-30

Observe the client's ability to harmonize and blend own voice with the group. M-25; F-32

Observe the client's ability to read music notation. If unable to read music notation, observe the client's ability to sing familiar songs from song lyrics. Teach the melody by rote to clients who cannot match the melody to the lyrics. M-31

S-4	Participates in a choir ($n3 = 1$; $n4 = 4$; $n5 = 5$; 6.67%)

Assign the clients to a choir. During choir rehearsal work on social skills, cooperation, listening to and following directions, singing correct parts in harmonization with the chorus, and voice blending and balancing. To provide a goal for the choir to work toward, arrange for the choir to perform four concerts per year. M-75; F-26-32

During warm-up activities work on patients blending their voices with the group. F-32

When Christmas approaches, arrange for the clients to go caroling from ward to ward with a hospital wide group. Observe the client's ability to function in moderate to large groups. F-30

S-5	Completes music questionnaire. Past singing performance is assessed by administering a music experience questionnaire ($n3 = 2$; $n4 = 2$; $n5 = 4$; 5.33%).

If the patient indicates a strong preference for singing, ask the patient to request a favorite song, then accompany as the patient sings the song. Observe vocal skill, lyric accuracy, and awareness of style and composer. M-26; F-50

If the patient indicates experience at singing in the church choir, play a patient-familiar church song (e.g., "Amazing Grace"). Observe the patient's vocal skills, such as awareness of key or the ability to sing in key. M-26

If the patient indicates a desire to learn songs, to sing, or to harmonize, provide group or individual voice lessons. F-50

S-6	Exhibits superior vocal skill ($n3 = 1$; $n4 = 2$; $n5 = 3$; 4%)

Patients who possess good vocal skill are good candidates for high status roles such as leading group singing. M-21; F-21

Enroll in voice lessons and expand knowledge of musical concepts and styles. F-36

S-7   Sings only one style of music (e.g., gospel, rock, or country, etc.) (n3 = 1; n4 = 2; n5 = 3; 4%)

Although the patient desires to learn other types of music, he or she doesn't because of continuously singing, for example, gospel. Make the singing of one gospel song at the end of the session contingent upon singing a variety of styles of music during the music therapy session. To promote generalization, give the patient a checklist listing various styles of music. Have the patient keep the checklist, checking the style of music each time he or she sings a song outside the music therapy session. Emphasize the necessity of singing a variety of styles, and ask the patient to bring the checklist to the next music therapy session for review. M-21;   F-21

Involve the patient in a sing-a-long group to increase exposure to a variety of styles of music. F-36

S-8   Demonstrates vocal range (n3 = 1; n4 = 2; n5 = 3; 4%)

Begin choir with vocal warm-ups. During warm-ups work at increasing vocal range. Increased vocal range will lead to increased confidence in singing activities. M-30; F-31

Do five-note ascending – descending vocal warm-up exercises starting on middle "C" and continuing through "G^1." Follow-up by singing a song in the range of the vocal warm-ups. F-31

S-9   Sings at least two lines of a song from memory (n3 = 1; n4 = 2; n5 = 3; 4%)

Ask the client to select a familiar song and to sing as much of the song as possible. NOTE: Transpose the song to the client's vocal range. M-41; F-25-41

S-10   Sings with correct pitch and rhythm (n3 = 2; n4 = 0; n5 = 2; 2.67%)

Observe the ability of the client to sing on pitch (The client chooses the song and the therapist accompanies on guitar or piano). M-30-40

S-11   Matches pitch (n3 = 1; n4 = 1; n5 = 2; 2.67%)

Observe whether the patient first listens to the pitch before attempting to match it. Model correct listening-matching response. Encourage the patient to practice listening before matching. M-30; F-30

S-12 Sings with appropriate dynamics (n3 = 1; n4 = 1; n5 = 2; 2.67%)

Teach the patients to blend vocally with others. Encourage the patients to listen to themselves, to each other, and to watch and sing according to the conductor's cues. M-30; F-31

S-13 The client requests voice lessons; expresses a desire to sing a solo of a favorite song (n3 = 1; n4 = 1; n5 = 2; 2.67%)

During voice lessons stress proper breathing, posture, and diction. M-75

Work on deep breathing, vocalization, song interpretation, and posture. Involve the client in a discussion of the lyrics. Encourage the client to sing with others in addition to singing solo. F-37

S-14 Demonstrates the ability to use the voice expressively; feels comfortable expressing oneself in song (n3 = 1; n4 = 1; n5 = 2; 2.67%)

Encourage the patient to use both body movement and vocal sounds to express a particular mood or emotion. M-40

Ask the client to pick a song to sing that she feels describes herself. F-20

S-15 Stays on task during singing activities; Indicates preference for singing (n3 = 0; n4 = 2; n5 = 2; 2.67%)

Give directives and ask questions to maintain on-task behavior (e.g., Ask the client to pick a song and then to sing the song. Ask the client questions relating to the song). F-20

Observe the patients on-task behavior during a sing-a-long (e.g., attention to song). F-60

S-16 Sings with breath control and appropriate intensity (n3 = 0; n4 = 1; n5 = 1; 1.33%)

Start by singing the chorus and one verse of a song (e.g., "Amazing Grace"). After a short break have the patient sing the chorus and another verse. Gradually increase the length of time singing without a break. F-31

S-17 Participates in toning exercises; demonstrates the ability to sing (match) the intonation sung by the leader of the toning activity (n3 = 0; n4 = 1; n5 = 1; 1.33%)

During toning exercises the group is instructed to follow the toning exercises of the leader. Each group member is given the opportunity to be the leader and to change the toning pattern. F-60

S-18 Sings both a cappella and with accompaniment ($n3 = 1$; $n4 = 0$; $n5 = 1$; 1.33%)

Ask the patient to sing a few bars of his favorite melody, after which the therapist joins in with an instrumental accompaniment (if possible). M-40

S-19 Demonstrates physiological aspects of vocalization ($n3 = 0$; $n4 = 1$; $n5 = 1$; 1.33%)

Observe quality of deep breathing, vocalization, or any need for speech correction. M-35

S-20 Sings lyrics to an entire song ($n3 = 0$; $n4 = 1$; $n5 = 1$; 1.33%)

Provide a piano accompaniment to a familiar song (e.g., "America") and encourage the patients to sing along. Note whether the patients can sing the words to the entire song. NOTE: Transpose the song to the client's vocal range. F-25

S-21 Sings lyrics to only phrases of songs ($n3 = 0$; $n4 = 1$; $n5 = 1$; 1.33%)

The therapist sings and plays the first half of the first phrase of a familiar song (e.g., "America"). Observe whether the patient can sing the lyrics to the remainder of the phrase while the therapist accompanies. NOTE: Transpose the song to the client's vocal range. F-25

S-22 Sings song lyrics in sequence ($n3 = 0$; $n4 = 1$; $n5 = 1$; 1.33%)

Ask the client to sing a familiar song, or to sing one line of a familiar song. Observe whether the lyrics are sung in the correct sequence. F-25

S-23 Performance anxiety; experiences anxiety about singing for others ($n3 = 1$; $n4 = 0$; $n5 = 1$; 1.33%)

Have the patient participate in a choir and schedule a concert every two to three months. Process performance anxiety feelings about each concert both before and after the concert. M-30

S-24 Expresses likes and dislikes about a song, or portions of the song ($n3 = 0$; $n4 = 1$; $n5 = 1$; 1.33%)

After singing songs discuss the song with the client. Note whether the client expresses both likes and dislikes about songs. F-35

PLAYING INSTRUMENTS (Combined, n = 65; 17.86%;
Male, n1 = 30; 46.15%; Female, n2 = 35; 53.85%)

<u>BEHAVIOR</u>   <u>MUSIC THERAPY INTERVENTION</u>

P-1   Demonstrates musical interest; may spontaneously play or attempt to play a
musical instrument; may or may not exhibit instrumental skill (n3 = 11;
n4 = 21; n5 = 32; 49.23%)

Increase the patient's musical skill. Help the client learn or re-learn a
musical skill. Provide regularly scheduled lessons on the patient's instrument of
choice (e.g., voice; piano; guitar; autoharp) in a group or one-to-one session.
Encourage daily practice. Increase peer acceptance, self-esteem, and confidence
by preparing the patient to perform for her peers (e.g., on the patient variety or
talent show or at a ward birthday party). Involve the patient in a combo to
promote small group interaction and peer acceptance. Encourage the patient to
continue using her musical skills after leaving the hospital. Suggest community
involvement in music after discharge from the hospital. Consider giving the
patient the opportunity to continue taking lessons from the therapist through
direct or community referral after release from the hospital. Prepare to focus
on primary psychotherapeutic (nonmusic) goals. M-21-30-30; F-21-30-
30-30-31-31-35-36-37-50-60

Provide the patient with a variety of musical instruments such as piano,
guitar, drums, autoharp, and xylophone. Assess the patient's ability to
play an instrument and to read music. M-40; F-36-30

Patients who demonstrate advanced performance ability on guitar or piano
may be auditioned for a coveted role, such as providing background music
for an exercise group. Giving a music performance can be a means of self
expression, or of gaining peer acceptance. M-21; F-21-39

Observe whether the patient plays an instrument well enough to derive
personal satisfaction and enjoyment from playing. M-30-60

If the patient wishes to learn the drum part of a recording, assist the
patient with listening analytically to the drum part of the recording.
M-51; F-51

Give the patient the opportunity to engage in solo experimentation on
preferred instruments (e.g., piano; drum). M-30; F-39

Involve the client in a band in which she can perform written as well as
improvised music. F-20

Assess the patient's present guitar playing ability by asking the patient if
they play guitar. If they indicate they do, give them a guitar and ask them
to play it. If the patient possesses at least minimal functional guitar
skill, encourage the patient to play the guitar during his free time while
in the hospital. Give the patient the opportunity to check out the guitar,

for use during his free time, by signing the "sign-out" or "instrument use" book. Monitor the sign-out book to determine whether the patient regularly checks out the guitar. M-40

Encourage the client to practice several songs they enjoy, then invite several peers or staff to come and listen to the client. M-31

Ask the client to practice with the therapist at least one hour twice a week. F-25

Ask the patient to identify the style of music she wishes to perform, and specific songs representative of the style. F-32

After performing selected music, the patient will evaluate her performance by identifying aspects of the music that was performed well and performed inaccurately. F-32

P-2   Demonstrates sufficient ability to perform solo or with an ensemble; maintains tempo and rhythm; plays dynamics (n3 = 5; n4 = 4; n5 = 9; 13.85%)

Observe the client's ability to perform with a group. Does the client use appropriate dynamic levels and tempo when performing with others? Does the client perform as a contributing member? M-30-85; F-60

Ask the client to play a prearranged accompaniment on Orff instruments as the therapist plays a pentatonic song incorporating two to three chords. Provide the client with different prearranged accompaniments for different Orff instruments. Observe the client's ability to stay in tempo with the pentatonic song. M-35-35; F-32

Ask the client to keep time to recorded music using their preferred rhythm instrument. Observe the client's ability to play rhythm instruments in time with the group. F-30; F-26

For the client who wishes to perform (play the drums) but has difficulty keeping a steady tempo, ask the client to play along with a radio or recording. Encourage the client to keep a steady beat. This activity helps to increase the person's self confidence that they can maintain a steady beat. M-31.

P-3   Performance anxiety; expresses desire to play for others but is fearful of solo playing; may be quiet and passive (n3 = 2; n4 = 4; n5 = 6; 9.23%)

Accompany the patient's performance. If the patient wishes to play, for example, a guitar solo during group sing-a-long, the therapist should accompany the patient's performance using a second guitar. M-51; F-51

During the patient's music lesson, have the patient to play for one or two peers. During combo rehearsal, have the patient play his or her instrument before the other group members. Have regularly scheduled combo concerts to enable the client to play for progressively large audiences. Process performance anxiety feelings about each concert both before and after the concert. M-30; F-20

Arrange for the patient to play for the music therapist at least twice a week. F-31

Observe the patient's willingness to play an instrument during group instrumental activities or to participate in a talent show or play. F-41

P-4 Performs in group ensemble for peers; expresses a desire to perform with the hospital performance group. (n3 = 4; n4 = 1; n5 = 5; 7.69%)

Involve the clients in an instrumental performance ensemble (e.g., hand bells; guitar). Have the group perform for facility and community functions. Emphasize group process. M-75-30

Involve the client in a group ensemble. Let the group take the responsibility for choosing the music and making all arrangements for the concert, which is to be given to their peers. If desired, arrangements may be made for certain clients to perform a vocal or instrumental solo during the concert. M-25

During combo rehearsal, teach the patients to hear chord changes by listening to recorded music. After identifying the chord changes, have them transcribe the music into lead sheet format. M-30

For patients who wish to learn piano, begin by teaching the patient to identify piano note names. Next teach right and left hand placements for playing simple I, IV, and V block chord progressions in various keys. F-31

P-5 Assess past instrumental performance by administering a music experience questionnaire (n3 = 3; n4 = 1; n5 = 4; 6.15%).

Client indicates any instrumental or vocal experience. M-30; F-30

If the client indicates experience at playing the guitar, give him a guitar and ask him to pluck the "D" string. M-26

If the client indicates he can read music, present him with music symbols and ask him to name the symbols (e.g., treble cleft; quarter note; common (4/4) time signature). M-26

P-6 Demonstrates the ability to imitate or repeat a rhythmic or melodic phrase (n3 = 2; n4 = 1; n5 = 3; 4.62%)

For rhythmic imitation, play a rhythmic pattern on a drum and ask the patient to repeat the pattern. For melodic imitation, play a melodic

pattern on an Orff instrument and ask the patient to repeat the pattern.
M-35-35;   F-32

P-7   Patient expresses a desire accompany own singing (n3 = 1; n4 = 1; n5 = 2;
3.08%)

For patients with little instrumental skill, provide autoharp or
omnichord instruction. M-51; F-51

P-8   Plays predetermined pattern on tone bells to create a familiar song (n3 = 1;
n4 = 1; n5 = 2; 3.08%)

Given a musical reference, ask the patient to play the melody of a
familiar song on tone bells. Determine whether the patient reads
notation, note letter names, or numbers. M-30; F-30

P-9   Participates in informal "jam session" (n3 = 1; n4 = 0; n5 = 1; 1.54%)

Have the clients attend sessions that allow them to interact with other clients
having varied levels of music skill. Encourage participants to learn songs from
each other as well as teach songs. The level of participation can be as simple as
playing a rhythm instrument or as complex as playing the guitar, drums, piano,
or a wind instrument. M-75

P-10 Performs a variety of musical styles; demonstrates tolerance for the music
preferences of others (n3 = 0; n4 = 1; n5 = 1; 1.54%)

Alternate patient preferred music with other styles of music. Ask the
patients to identify different elements of the music, such as the melody,
bass, and percussion. F-31

IMPROVISING MUSIC (Combined, n = 54; 14.83%; Male, n1 = 22; 40.74%;
Female, n2 = 32; 59.26%)

BEHAVIOR   MUSIC THERAPY INTERVENTION

I-1   Plays Orff and rhythm instruments during free or structured improvisation
sessions (n3 = 6; n4 = 12; n5 = 18; 33.33%)

Observe the client's quality of participation in group improvisation (e.g.,
trades instruments with peers upon request; follows auditory cues by
ceasing to play instrument when accompaniment or leader stops playing;
cooperates and follows directions; plays at appropriate times;
demonstrates creativity; listens to others and plays as a group member
rather than as an individual; works with group to create finished
product). Observe whether each client improvises a pattern, or

contributes a song or song line, a thought, a word, or an idea to be depicted.   M-25-41;   F-25-35-39-41-65

Ask the patient to use percussion accessories to provide an improvisation to a recording. M-51; F-37-51

Observe the client's instrumental facility (e.g., the number of instruments the client is able to play and the quality of improvisation). M-25;   F-65

Observe the client's quality of free improvisation on Orff and rhythm instruments. Does the patient demonstrate flexibility and creativity? Is the patient able to be creative while experimenting with rhythm and tone?   F-30-39

Ask the patient to choose two or three chord progressions on which to base a guitar improvisation. M-32

Given a harmonic structure as an accompaniment, the patient is able to improvise at least a 12-bar melody on her preferred melodic instrument. F-35

Given instrument of choice, ask the patient to choose an ostinato pattern on which to perform with the group. M-32

During structured improvisation, encourage the patient to improvise on an instrument to an underlying ostinato (e.g., one client or the group plays the ostinato while another patient plays an improvisation). F-25

I-2   Expresses feelings and expressiveness through music improvisation; demon-strates the ability to play the sound of a feeling. ($n3 = 3$; $n4 = 4$; $n5 = 7$; 12.96%)

Observe whether the patient can convey emotional responses through a sound medium. Ask the patient to play an instrument in a manner that expresses her mood. After the patient finishes playing, ask her to verbalize her mood. M-30; F-60

Ask the client to choose an instrument that matches a mood or a day she has experienced (e.g., "Choose an instrument that reminds you of _____."). Ask the client to play the instrument. Discuss with the client how she felt when playing, and if it was a sound she could modify. F-31

Ask the patient to select an instrument of choice, then communicate his current affect or feeling by expressively playing the instrument. M-40

Have the client express feelings by using instruments to create original sound effects and to match specific emotions. M-35

Give the client a card with a specific feeling written on it. Ask the client to play the sound of the feeling on a rhythm instrument. F-60

Using the pentatonic scale and Orff instruments, assign a patient to improvise appropriate background music during the recitation of a poem. The music should be appropriate to the mood and content of the poem. F-39

I-3   Maintains ostinato pattern; plays rhythmically; keeps a steady beat ($n3 = 3$; $n4 = 2$; $n5 = 5$; 9.26%)

Play a one or two measure rhythmic pattern on a drum and observe the client's ability to imitate the pattern. M-25

The patient chooses an ostinato pattern and establishes the tempo. F-32

The therapist plays "La Bamba" on the guitar or piano while the client creates a rhythmic accompaniment to the music using the claves. The therapist also may assign the client to play a set, or structured rhythmic accompaniment throughout the song (e.g., **C** | || | |). M-26

Using a rhythm instrument activity, the leader plays an ostinato rhythmic pattern on a drum. The group members join in one-by-one, each imitating the leaders rhythmic pattern on their instrument. M-35; F-32

I-4   Improvises a rhythm or melody over a rhythmic or melodic ostinato pattern ($n3 = 1$; $n4 = 4$; $n5 = 5$; 9.26%)

Using Orff instruments, present a rhythmic and/or melodic ostinato pattern and ask the patient to improvise a melody over the pattern. M-35; F-32-35

Teach the patient a melodic pattern on her preferred instrument. F-32

Observe the patient's ability to play a counter beat, an alternating beat, and her own rhythmic pattern in the presence of a steady beat played by the therapist. F-35

I-5   Feels inferior musically; the client is convinced she cannot play music; exhibits excessive fear of musical failure and fear of musical participation; exhibits low self-confidence and low self-esteem; makes negative statements such as "I can't" ($n3 = 2$; $n4 = 2$; $n5 = 4$; 7.41%)

Uses improvisational techniques to provide the client with positive and successful musical experiences (e.g., prepare the client to perform an ostinato part). M-40; F-50

Involve the client in structured improvisation. M-40

Use nontraditional instrumental techniques and/or the pentatonic scale to facilitate success (e.g., Set the electronic piano or keyboard to play a rhythmic accompaniment. Using the pentatonic scale, have the client improvise a melody to the rhythmic accompaniment by playing the black keys on the keyboard or by playing a melodic percussion instrument such as the xylophone). Encourage peer acceptance and praise of the performance. F-30

I-6   Demonstrates preference for improvisational instruments (n3 = 1; n4 = 2; n5 = 3; 5.56%)

Given improvisational instruments for ensemble playing, each client will choose her preferred instrument. M-41; F-32-41

I-7   Demonstrates the ability to musically imitate, alternate, and initiate during improvisation (n3 = 2; n4 = 1; n5 = 3; 5.56%)

Observe whether the client initiates verbal or nonverbal participation with the therapist or a peer. Using rhythm instruments, try a mirroring to music activity in which the therapist or a peer leads and the client follows. Repeat the activity with the client leading and the therapist or peer following. NOTE: A two measure improvised rhythm pattern is suggested. Observe how many times the leader must present the rhythm pattern before the client can correctly repeat or echo the pattern.
  M-25; F-30

Ask the patient to engage in musical mirroring, followed by musical conversation with the therapist. M-40

I-8   The patient expresses a desire to improvise at the piano (n3 = 1; n4 = 2; n5 = 3; 5.56%)

For patients with little piano background, involve the patient in a pentatonic duet (the therapist improvises on the black keys in one register of the keyboard while the patient improvises on the black keys in another register). M-51; F-51

Provide experience at unstructured, guided improvisation. Have the patients to play a pentatonic improvisation on the black keys of the piano. Suggest a scene (e.g., a thunderstorm) for the patients to create or represent through their improvisation. F-25

I-9   Expresses creativity during group improvisation; creatively explores instrument (n3 = 1; n4 = 1; n5 = 2; 3.70%)

The client will improvise at least two varied rhythms, without prompts, while playing the hand drum during group improvisation. M-30

Ask the client to nonverbally "say something" while playing the xylophone to the therapist's accompaniment. The client may use only xylophone playing and nonverbal gestures to communicate. F-25

I-10 Feels at ease with playing a variety of sounds on different Orff instruments ($n3 = 0$; $n4 = 1$; $n5 = 1$; 1.85%)

Teach the client a simple ostinato pattern on her chosen instrument. After the client learns the pattern, ask her to vary the sound while maintaining the same pattern. Repeat until the client plays three different versions of the same pattern on a variety of Orff instruments. F-31

I-11 Leads or conducts group improvisation sessions ($n3 = 0$; $n4 = 1$; $n5 = 1$; 1.85%)

Ask the client to use the baton to indicate changes in musical characteristics such as dynamics and tempo. F-35

I-12 "Hears" chord changes ($n3 = 1$; $n4 = 0$; $n5 = 1$; 1.85%)

The therapist provides the client with a guitar so that both the therapist and the client have a guitar. The client and therapist then play their guitars while singing a familiar song. Observe whether the client changes chords at the appropriate times (NOTE: The therapist may need to use nontraditional, simplified guitar techniques, or restrict the client's role to providing a one note accompaniment on the xylophone, bass keyboard, or guitar). M-26

I-13 Interacts with other group members while improvising ($n3 = 1$; $n4 = 0$; $n5 = 1$; 1.85%)

Ask the client to improvise a response to an improvised statement made by another group member. M-35

I-14 Improvises movements to music (see "Participates in unstructured creative movement to music" under "Locomotor Movement To Music")

LOCOMOTOR MOVEMENT TO MUSIC (Combined, n = 31; 8.52%;
Male, n1 = 8; 25.81%; Female, n2 = 23; 74.19%)

<u>BEHAVIOR</u>   <u>MUSIC THERAPY INTERVENTION</u>

LM-1 Dances to music (e.g., ballroom; square; folk); participates in structured dance; participates in dance mixer or social dance; may demonstrate previous dancing experience (n3 = 2; n4 = 6; n5 = 8; 25.81%)

Play dance music and invite the patients to participate in dancing.
Observe whether patients participate independently or with prompts.
F-35-41

Ask the client with prior dancing experience to assist the therapist in teaching a dance (e.g., a square dance) to the group. M-21; F-21

Play patient preferred music, or play "patient era" music if the musical preferences of the patient are unknown. Instrumental "dance era" music is recommended. THERAPIST NOTE: Ballroom dancing is the style of dance most preferred by my patients. M-40

Observe whether the patient asks a peer to dance during coed dance (socialization) activities. F-35

Observe whether participation in dance or movement activities reduces the client's symptoms of tension. F-30

Observe the client's quality of rhythmic movement while she is dancing.
F-36

LM-2 Participates in structured creative movement to music; imitates or mirrors movements to music (n3 = 2; n4 = 3; n5 = 5; 16.13%)

Ask the clients to imitate a leader in creative movement activities.
The clients take turns being the leader, or the therapist can be the leader.
M-25;   F-25-26

Divide the clients into pairs. Ask the first client of each pair to move to the music while the second client imitates the movement. Follow-up by having the clients switch roles (i.e., the second client assumes the first client's role and the first client assumes the second client's role) so the imitation skills of all clients can be observed. M-25; F-65

LM-3 Participates in unstructured creative movement to music; spontaneously moves to music (n3 = 0; n4 = 4; n5 = 4; 12.90%)

Assess the patient's spontaneous movement to music. Note any indications of psychiatric problems. F-26-37

Play music and encourage the patients to move independently to the music. Provide imagery for the patients to create and represent in their movements. Imagery, music, and movement may be used to energize the clients (e.g., Ask the clients to imitate African dance movements to the song, "The Rhythm is Gonna [sic] Get You" by Miami Sound Machine). F-25

Ask the clients to select a movement that expresses something about themselves, and which will "pass" their energy. Observe their movements to previously selected recorded music. F-30

LM-4 Moves in rhythm to music ($n3 = 1$; $n4 = 2$; $n5 = 3$; 9.68%)

Have the client mirror the therapist's movements. Use appropriate prompting if necessary. M-25

Involve the client in a music exercise or dance group in which the client can learn basic movements or dance steps to music. F-20

Use structured movement exercise to rhythmic music with patients who have difficulty moving rhythmically or difficulty controlling voluntary movements. F-30

LM-5 Participates in aerobics ($n3 = 0$; $n4 = 3$; $n5 = 3$; 9.68%)

Involve the client in a music exercise group to increase physical movement, self-esteem, and self-image. F-20

Involve the client in aerobic exercise to music. F-41

Involve the client in choosing the music for dance aerobics and water aerobics. F-36

LM-6 Maintains the tempo of the music given directed gross motor movements ($n3 = 1$; $n4 = 1$; $n5 = 2$; 6.45%)

Play a recording with a tempo of approximately 60 beats per minute and observe the client's ability to do aerobic exercises in rhythm to the music. M-26; F-26

LM-7 Integrates and performs a structured movement pattern to music given verbal directives by the therapist ($n3 = 1$; $n4 = 1$; $n5 = 2$; 6.45%)

Client follows dance sequence to instrumental music. M-25

Design the movement pattern to serve the patient's physical and expressive needs. F-37

LM-8 Participates in creative dance and body language ($n3 = 0$; $n4 = 1$; $n5 = 1$; 3.23%)

Involve the client in a body language group to increase physical movement, self-esteem, and self-image. F-20

LM-9 Awareness of personal space or body limits during movement to music ($n3 = 1$; $n4 = 0$; $n5 = 1$; 3.23%)

Observe whether the patient verbally identifies and physically responds to personal space limits (e.g., does not intrude upon the space of others; does not constantly bump into others). M-32

LM-10 Leads group in simple, repetitive creative movement ($n3 = 0$; $n4 = 1$; $n5 = 1$; 3.23%)

Observe the patient leading the group in movement to music. F-32

LM-11 Feels comfortable with structured movement activity ($n3 = 0$; $n4 = 1$; $n5 = 1$; 3.23%)

Use a game involving movement to music to assist clients in feeling comfortable with structured movement activities (e.g., Play the game, "Who Started The Motion." This game involves structured movement to music. F-65

COMPOSING MUSIC (Combined, $n = 18$; 4.95%; Male, $n1 = 7$; 38.89%; Female, $n2 = 11$; 61.11%)

BEHAVIOR   MUSIC THERAPY INTERVENTION

C-1   Client participates in lyric writing; participates in setting lyrics to music ($n3 = 5$; $n4 = 9$; $n5 = 14$; 77.78%)

The goal is to get a tangible "black and white" copy of the client's true feelings. Does the client write lyrics that reflect appropriate self awareness, emotion, and contact with the environment? Does the client give suggestions for lyrics based on her own thoughts and feelings? M-35-30;   F-39-60

During group song writing, give each group member a work sheet and ask each person to contribute to the parody. The melody used may be a familiar song (e.g., "Greatest Love of All"). F-60-65

Observe whether each client contributes a line to the song, a thought, a word, or an idea to be depicted. F-39

Have each client make up their own lyrical verse to the melody of a familiar song such as "Kum Bah Yah." F-26

During lyric writing, have each patient create one line of lyrics. F-31

Observe the quality of participation. Observe whether the client communicates thoughts about lyrics and melody to the group, demonstrates creativity and flexibility, and works with the entire group in shaping the product. F-39

Involve the client in writing lyrics in Blues form. The therapist uses a guitar to sing with the client, lyrics already written, and to prompt the client into thinking of and trying new lyrics. M-30

With the therapist's assistance, the client decides which melody and chord progression best expresses the lyrics (which are reflective of the client's feelings). M-35

Select a melody that is unknown to the client then teach the client to hum the melody. After the client learns the melody ask the client to compose lyrics to the melody. Give necessary assistance. M-35

Given a song (e.g., "I Am A Rock") with certain key lyrics deleted, have the client to fill in the missing words (blanks) with words that describe herself (For example, in the chorus: "I am _____ ., I am _____ ." F-39

C-2   Client expresses a desire to compose, sing or play own compositions
($n3 = 2$; $n4 = 1$; $n5 = 3$; 16.67%)

Therapist provides coaching sessions with performance upon termination of sessions. M-21; F-21

During a one-to-one session, assist the client at composing lyrics and music. Encourage a possible performance for peers and staff. M-31

C-3   Demonstrates the ability to learn a newly composed song by rote ($n3 = 0$; $n4 = 1$; $n5 = 1$; 5.56%)

During group song writing, the clients learn to sing each phrase of the newly completed song by rote (e.g., the therapist sings a phrase, followed by the clients singing the same phrase in imitation of the therapist). F-60

NONLOCOMOTOR MOVEMENT TO MUSIC (Combined, n = 9; 2.47%;
Male, n1 = 5; 55.56%; Female, n2 = 4; 44.45%)

<u>BEHAVIOR</u>   <u>MUSIC THERAPY INTERVENTION</u>

NL-1   Imitates movements to music (n3 = 2; n4 = 1; n5 = 3; 33.33%)

Use scarves to create a mirroring experience for clients. Divide the clients into pairs and give each client a scarf. Ask first client of each pair to move a scarf to the music while the second client uses a scarf to imitate the movement. Follow-up by having the clients to switch roles (i.e., the second client assumes the first client's role and the first client assumes the second client's role) so the imitation skills of all clients can be observed. M-41; F-41

Select one patient to lead the group in a creative movement activity. Observe whether each group member follows the leader's movements to music. M-32

NL-2   Changes movement in response to music (n3 = 1; n4 = 1; n5 = 2; 22.22%)

Use a parachute activity in which short musical excerpts are used to accompany the movement of the parachute. Ask the client to respond to different musical styles by moving the parachute in a manner that reflects the mood, rhythm and tempo of the music. M-41; F-41

NL-3   Taps fingers on legs or tray, taps toes, or claps to music (n3 = 1; n4 = 1; n5 = 2; 22.22%)

Play patient-preferred music, or "patient-era" music if the patient's musical preferences are unknown. Lively instrumental music is recommended because music with lyrics may be distracting. M-40

Observe rhythmic response to music during group or one-to-one session (e.g., tapping fingers, toes, or clapping). F-36

NL-4   Follows and maintains pulse; claps in rhythm to the beat of the music (n3 = 1; n4 = 1; n5 = 2; 22.22%)

Play recorded music, or the piano, and observe whether the patient can clap his hands to the beat of the music. M-25

The therapist models the rhythmic beat (e.g., finger snaps or claps) and the patient continues independently. Observe the patient's ability to follow the therapist and maintain the tempo. F-32

CODE: N = Total number of music therapy interventions submitted for Adults.

$N1$ = Number of music therapy interventions submitted for adult males for all assessment areas. % = Percentage of N

$N2$ = Number of music therapy interventions submitted for adult females. % = Percentage of N

n = Total number of music therapy interventions submitted for a particular area of assessment. % = Percentage of N.

$n1$ = Number of music therapy interventions submitted for males within a particular area of assessment. % = Percentage of n.

$n2$ = Number of music therapy interventions submitted for females within a particular area of assessment. % = Percentage of n.

$n3$ = Number of music therapy interventions submitted for males for a specific problem. % = Percentage of $n5$.

$n4$ = Number of music therapy interventions submitted for females for a specific problem. % = Percentage of $n5$.

$n5$ = Total number of music therapy interventions submitted for the specific music behavior. % = Percentage of n.

The number(s) after each intervention (e.g., 36) refers to the mean **Global Assessment of Functioning Scale** (*GAF Scale*) (*DSM-III-R*, 1987) score of clients for whom the intervention was designed. One score was given by each music therapist specifying the intervention (e.g., "25-30-36" indicates the particular intervention was submitted by three music therapists, and that the intervention is used with clients having the three indicated GAF scores). The *GAF* scores are preceded by an "M" or an "F," indicating whether the intervention was written for male clients or female clients.

ASSESSMENT AREA

LISTENING TO MUSIC (n = 30; 28.85%)

<u>BEHAVIOR</u>   <u>MUSIC THERAPY INTERVENTION</u>

L-1   Demonstrates awareness of a variety of styles of music rather than a single style (e.g., prefers only the latest teen-age "sensation"); demonstrates musical knowledge; can discuss musical likes and dislikes using musical terms; tolerates the music preferences of others rather than becoming aggressive toward others because of their musical preferences; is not opinionated about musical preferences to the extent of being intolerant of the preferences of others; gains awareness of the discipline of composition; learns to respect both past and present composers (n_1 = 11; 36.67%)

At the beginning of the session, greet the clients with an opening song. 35

Conduct a "rate a record" session in which each group member rates their preference for each group member's chosen song. 50

Ask the clients to each choose a song that best describes themselves and to play the song for the group. Follow-up with a discussion of why the song describes the client, and why the client likes the song. 50

If the client prefers only one type of music, conduct a lyric analysis. Ask the client to describe the meaning of the lyrics and to tell why she likes the music. 45

Construct a music listening schedule to provide each patient the opportunity to listen to their preferred music. 45

Listen to a variety of music. After each composition is played, analyze the style of music, musical form, the rhythm, the chord structure, and whether the composition was a vocal or instrumental performance. Have each client explain why they did or did not like the music. Note whether the preference expressed was because of the musical characteristics or because of another reason. 43-40-50

Play a variety of music for the adolescent music therapy group. After each selection is played ask a group member to give feedback relating to the music. Encourage each patient to give positive feed back, or to give at least one positive comment for every negative comment. 40

Study, with the students, the lives and works of famous composers. Listen to the compositions and assist the students in understanding what each composer is "trying to say" musically. 50

Without playing the music, give the clients the lyrics to a variety of unfamiliar music and ask them to pick out the lyrics of a song that is meaningful, or that relates to their life. After discussing the lyrics, have them listen to the music. Foster the realization that songs they don't normally listen to can be meaningful to them. 40

L-2   Demonstrates musical preferences (n^1 = 9; 30.00%)

During "free listening" let each patient choose their favorite song to play for the group then explain their choice. 50

Ask the patients to bring to the session taped music that expresses their opinion about a topic chosen by the group. Observe each client's music preferences as well as their tolerance for the music preferences of others. 31

Observe whether the client makes "healthy" music choices, or "unhealthy" music choices that reinforce inappropriate behavior. Conduct lyric analysis to examine the client's music preferences. 46

During music appreciation, conduct the "rate-a-record" activity in which each client rates their musical preferences. Develop the patient's awareness of how listening to specific types of music can influence a person socially, mentally and physically. 46

Involve the client in a "rate-a-record" session during which recordings are played, then rated and discussed by each client. 40

Given an extensive list of songs, ask the patient to choose a song from the list to play for the group. Follow-up by asking the patient why she likes the song and what the song means to her. 40

Ask each client to bring a song to play for the group at the next session. 3 5

Play a variety of music and ask the clients to state their opinion of the music. 50

THERAPIST NOTE: The adolescent's "rock music world" is highly significant in regard to affective and interpersonal issues. 50

L-3   Listens to or uses music for own physical and emotional relaxation; develops an awareness of various classical and jazz styles used for relaxation (n1 = 2; 6.67%)

In the presence of relaxing background music, ask the clients to relax, to surround themselves by their favorite color, and to create a "safe place" in their imagination. 50

Conduct progressive muscle relaxation and guided imagery to jazz or classical background music. 40

L-4   Demonstrates the ability to associate affect with corresponding music; verbalizes perceived mood of preferred music; identifies the mood of the music (n1 = 1; 3.33%)

Ask the group members to bring to the music therapy session four songs, each corresponding to a specific feeling, such as "happy," "sad," "mad," or "scared." Play the songs and have the group discuss which emotion category would be appropriate for each song. 36

L-5   Exhibits interest in new areas of music (n1 = 1; 3.33%)

Conduct a discussion of current musical trends, new innovations in musical equipment, and the latest music technology. 31

L-6   Chooses music that expresses own social, political, interpersonal, and religious viewpoints (n1 = 1; 3.33%)

Ask the patients to bring to the session taped music which expresses their opinion about a topic chosen by the group. 31

L-7   Demonstrates the ability to identify differences in timbre, pitch, and the overall mood of music (n1 = 1; 3.33%)

Ask the client to draw or write while focusing on a feeling in the presence of background music. 50

L-8   Develops confidence in the validity of own musical interpretations (n1 = 1; 3.33%)

Have the students listen to an instrumental piece, then write and discuss their thoughts, images, and ideas of the meaning of the piece. 40

L-9   Listens to the lyrics of music (n1 = 1; 3.33%)

During lyric discussion, study the lives of both past and present composers. Study the songs or works of composers who were successful despite overwhelming odds and great obstacles. 50

L-10 Concentrates on entire music composition while listening; attends to music ($n1 = 1$;   3.33%)

> Observe the client's ability to concentrate on, attend to, or listen to music compositions during music listening. If the client experiences apparent difficulty, ask the client to listen to one particular musical element (e.g., a particular music instrument). It may be necessary to start with listening assignments of short duration, then to gradually lengthen the duration of the assignments as the client masters them. 40

PLAYING INSTRUMENTS ($n = 19$; 18.27%)

<u>BEHAVIOR</u>   <u>MUSIC THERAPY INTERVENTION</u>

P-1   Client demonstrates an interest in music; expresses a desire to play an instrument ($n1 = 8$; 42.12%)

> Involve the patients in group activities where various aspects of music are demonstrated. For example, provide demonstrations of keyboards, the guitar, recording techniques, drums (trap set), string bass, electronic and computerized musical equipment, and MIDI. Conduct structured rhythmic and melodic activities using the instruments. Note whether the client follows instructions in the proper use of instruments. 31-40-50
>
> Involve the client in a rhythmic activity using Kodály notation. 50
>
> Provide clients with the opportunity to take lessons on instruments they are interested in. Encourage daily practice. 31-45
>
> Establish goals that are motivating and challenging. Grade students weekly on progress toward these goals (e.g., David will play "Stairway to Heaven" on guitar; David will play the "C" major and "G" major scales three octaves). 50
>
> Work individually with each student to assure success in meeting their musical goals. Also, provide a much needed "therapeutic ear." For example during individual lessons, David, a student, may speak about suicide. Discuss this openly with David and quickly get professional help for him. 50

P-2   Plays instrument for others; possesses music skill, talent, or training
(n1 = 6; 31.58%)

Invite the client to perform for the therapist or the group. Observe the
client's ability to control possible performance anxiety. If performance
anxiety is manifest, give the client additional experience at performing
before other group members during the music therapy session. The
group performances should be the decision of the client. If the client has
the skill to perform but does not desire to perform for others, then the
music therapist should increase the client's self confidence during
individual music lessons. Performance material could include music
learned from private lessons with the music therapist. Discuss with the
client any feelings of performance anxiety both before and after her
recital. 31-50

Ask the patient to bring to the therapy session music that they have
previously learned. Observe degree of musical training or talent. 50

Provide the patient with an opportunity to play an instrument in the
talent show or other special events. 51

Involve the patient in an ensemble. Have the ensemble rehearse a
patient-preferred song such as "Right Stuff" by New Kids on the Block.
After learning the song, have the ensemble first perform for one or two
staff, and then for the hospital dance. 46

Invite each student to audition for the "Student of the Month" assembly in
which the school recognizes academic and behavioral achievement. The
auditions require intensive preparation. Appoint a panel of two staff and
two students to judge the auditions. If three of the four judges accept the
audition as passing, the student gets to give the "Student of the Month"
performance. 50

P-3   Participates in a group ensemble; cooperates and blends with the group;
demonstrates musical sensitivity; is not excessively demanding (e.g., must always be the
soloist) (n1 = 2; 10.53%)

Have the ensemble perform a preferred composition, such as "Right
Stuff" by New Kids on the Block. Let the clients take turns directing the
ensemble. Note whether each client is able to direct the tempo, dynamics
and the soloists, to identify musical elements, and to give and receive
suggestions for an improved performance. 40-46

P-4   Critiques musical performance; gives and receives constructive criticism or
opinions (n1 = 1; 5.26%)

Following a live or recorded performance of the group ensemble, prompt
the patients to express their opinions about the performance. 40

P-5 Demonstrates rhythmic ability sufficient to play an instrument ($n1 = 1$; 5.26%)

> Involve the client in a rhythmic imitation activity in which the therapist plays a short rhythm and the client imitates. If the client successfully imitates, do a follow-up activity in which the therapist plays a 12-bar blues pattern while the client provides a rhythmic accompaniment. 35

P-6 Develops respect for various musical styles by participating in instrumental ensembles ($n1 = 1$; 5.26%)

> Have the group instrumental ensemble play a variety of music, such as African music, blues, gospel, spirituals, and jazz. 40

IMPROVISING MUSIC ($n = 17$; 16.35%)

BEHAVIOR   MUSIC THERAPY INTERVENTION

I-1 Varies improvisation by changing the pitch, the rhythm, and the volume ($n1 = 4$; 23.53%)

> Observe the client's ability to imitate changes in pitch, rhythm and volume while improvising. Play "Musical Duets" in which one client leads the improvisation while the other client imitates. 50
>
> Give the patient a xylophone or metallophone and ask the patient to play any notes she wishes to play as the therapist accompanies with a rhythmic ostinato. Note the range of notes the patient plays. 46
>
> Ask the patients to each choose an instrument. The therapist then begins an improvisation. Each group member, upon feeling comfortable enough, joins in the improvisation using their chosen instrument. Observe the quality of each patient's improvisation in terms of melody, pitch, rhythm, intensity, and creativity. 50
>
> Given melodic Orff instruments with only the bars to the pentatonic scale, ask the client to play three different instruments in three different ways (without being destructive) while the therapist plays an ostinato pattern on a bass instrument. The total performance should last approximately two minutes. Observe the client's ability to perform contrasting improvisations. 46

I-2 Demonstrates the ability to improvise on a melodic instrument within a rhythmic structure; able to improvise rhythmic patterns ($n1 = 3$; 17.65%)

> Have the patient improvise on a metallophone while the group provides an ostinato rhythmic accompaniment on percussion instruments. This

condition also may be implemented utilizing a variety of percussion instruments. 40-43

During improvisation, observe the patient's ability to improvise on progressively more complex harmonic structures (e.g., pentatonic, blues, rock 'n roll, or popular). 40

I-3 Demonstrates awareness of the musical responses of other group members during improvisational activities; listens to the improvisations of other group members to produce a blending and cohesive sound during group improvisation (n1 = 2; 11.77%)

During group improvisation ask one patient to conduct or lead the group improvisation. Observe the improvisations of each group member. 50

During structured improvisation, ask the patients to do a group improvisation of a word or a feeling. 50

I-4 Demonstrates an interest in playing music instruments; realizes instant success (n1 = 2; 11.77%)

Arrange for the client to improvise on a variety of instruments. 50

Ask the students to improvise various feelings or situations on their preferred instruments. Encourage interest and motivation by letting the students discover they can experiment and improvise on instruments without having to take lessons. 40

I-5 Demonstrates the ability to improvise on the pentatonic scale (n1 = 2; 11.77%)

Provide the client with the notes of the pentatonic scale using the xylophone or tone bells. Prompt the client to improvise on the pentatonic scale (e.g., "Play some different five-note patterns."). 35-50

I-6 Improvises on the blues scale; discovers a means of self expression by playing, singing, and improvising in blues style (n1 = 1; 5.88%)

Teach the clients the basic structure of the blues, then have them improvise both instrumentally and vocally in blues form and style. 40

I-7 Demonstrates the ability to create improvisations representative of moods (n1 = 1; 5.88%)

Ask the client to improvise a current feeling. 50

I-8 Demonstrates the ability to improvise with one other person (n1 = 1; 5.88%)

Select two patients and give each a xylophone with only the tone bars forming the pentatonic scale. Ask the clients to work together at improvising a musical composition. 43

I-9   Improvises musically rather than randomly playing notes on an instrument ($n1$ = 1; 5.88%)

> Introduce to the client simple rhythmic and melodic patterns. Suggest and demonstrate simple improvisatory techniques. 45

I-10 Improvises movement to music (see "Participates in unstructured creative movement to music" under "Locomotor Movement To Music")

SINGING (n =17; 16.35%)

BEHAVIOR   MUSIC THERAPY INTERVENTION

S-1   Observe singing skills such as the ability to match pitch and follow rhythms ($n1$ = 4; 23.53%)

> Conduct a sing-a-long. Observe the client singing. 50

> Play middle "C" on the piano and ask the patient to sing the pitch. 46

> Note each patient's most comfortable pitch. Ask each patient to sing their most comfortable pitch, then match the pitch using the piano. 46

> Observe the patient's ability to sing a melody with rhythmic and melodic accuracy. Ask the patient to sing a familiar popular song while the therapist plays the melody. 46

S-2   Sings solo in front of group ($n1$ = 3; 17.65%)

> Conduct the "Alphabet Game." Ask the clients to name a song for each letter of the alphabet. Give bonus points to clients for singing a song phrase or a song before the group. 50

> Provide the patient with an opportunity to sing in the talent show or other special events. 40-51

S-3   Blends with group when singing; does not sing louder than other group members ($n1$ = 3; 17.65%)

> Videotape the "Music Show" rehearsal during each music therapy session. When viewing the videotape, assist clients in understanding the importance of blending with the other group members and in presenting a group effort. 36

During choir rehearsal, encourage the patients to listen to their own singing, to each other, and to follow or match the conductor's cues. 31

Observe the client singing a solo or singing with the group. 40

S-4	Sings with adequate loudness; does not sing with a low inaudible voice. $(n1 = 2; 11.77\%)$

Involve the client, who does not sing loudly enough, in a chorus or in group singing. The client may sing as loud as the other group members, which may in turn strengthen the client's voice. 40-36

S-5	Sings with a vocal tone that is not too breathy $(n1 = 1; 5.88\%)$

If the client's vocal tone is too breathy when singing, tape record the client's singing each session to stimulate her awareness of how she sounds. 36

S-6	Sings in tune with a pleasing timbre $(n1 = 1; 5.88\%)$

Observe the client singing a solo or singing with the group. 40

S-7	Sings with proper diction $(n1 = 1; 5.88\%)$

Involve the client in group singing in which the group members are called upon to sing impromptu solos. 36

S-8	Demonstrates expanded vocal range resulting in increased confidence in singing ability $(n1 = 1; 5.88\%)$

Conduct vocal warm-ups at the beginning of each choir rehearsal to establish or expand singing range. 31

S-9	Sings with a choir $(n1 = 1; 5.88\%)$

Give patients the opportunity to sing in a choir. Schedule the choir to perform every two or three months. Discuss with the choir feelings about performance anxiety both before and after each choir concert. 31

COMPOSING MUSIC (n = 17; 16.35%)

<u>BEHAVIOR</u>   <u>MUSIC THERAPY INTERVENTION</u>

C-1   Demonstrates the ability to write music including lyrics and melody; composes and performs own music; demonstrates the ability to compose lyrics and phrases that fit the rhythm of the song; is able to use music composition as a means of self expression (n1 = 4; 23.53%)

Assist the patients in writing lyrics that are based on a topic chosen by the music therapist. Following a discussion of musical style, have the group choose a style, then write a melody in the chosen style that matches the lyrics. Emotionally disturbed students often have "more to say" emotionally than do "normal" students. 40-43-50

During group song writing, write a song, lyrics, and rhythmic accompaniment which is based on current treatment or unit issues. 50

C-2   Develops the ability to use lyric writing as a means of self expression; writes own lyrics (n1 = 3; 17.65%)

Introduce various lyric or song writing techniques, such as fill-in-the-blank, blues form, parody, and song writing. THERAPIST NOTE: One of our students wrote lyrics meaningful enough to be reviewed by the American Psychiatric Association (APA). 40-40-50

C-3   Participates in writing song parodies (n1 = 2; 11.76%)

After identifying a patient-preferred song, individualize the song by having the patient either rewrite all the lyrics or rewrite only part of the lyrics (e.g., rewrite a key word for each phrase: "Fill in the blank."); Using the melody of a familiar song, have the patient write new lyrics which describe herself and her experiences. 43-46

C-4   Participates in music composition activities in which compositions are based on pictures, themes, or abstract objects or symbols (e.g., lightning; water; the Sun; an exclamation mark [!]; unfamiliar instrumental music) (n1 = 2; 11.76%)

Have the clients listen to a recording used for guided imagery. After listening to the composition, have the clients elaborate on and develop the guided imagery composition using Orff instruments, chants, movement, and music composition techniques. 40

Given a theme such as "Stay In School," have the group compose a composition or rap based on the theme. Select the theme within specified guidelines, create the rhymes or raps, add percussion, perform, and record. 40

C-5 Experiences difficulty with composing song lyrics because of the inability to respond rhythmically (n_1 = 2; 11.76%)

Assist the client with composing and establishing a rhythm. Once the rhythm is learned, assist the client in creating a rap song based on the rhythm (e.g., My name is _____ . I'm here to say _____ today. [to an accompanying rhythm]).
36-46

C-6 Demonstrates respect for a variety of musical styles (n_1 = 1; 5.88%)

Have the students write a song (lyrics and music) combining two styles of music. 40

C-7 Has trouble rhyming or thinking of lyrics for phrases because of a poor vocabulary (n_1 = 1; 5.88%)

Play a song that can be used as a parody. Give the client a copy of the song lyrics and assist the client in deleting certain parts of speech, such as the nouns, adjectives, or clauses. The client then substitutes new words for the deleted words, changing the meaning of the song. 36

C-8 Demonstrates the ability to use imagination to create music productions (n_1 = 1; 5.88%)

Involve the clients in creating their own music video and radio productions. 40

C-9 Demonstrates the ability to organize sounds into music (n_1 = 1; 5.88%)

Let each group member choose an instrument to play, and let one patient serve as the conductor. The conductor's responsibility is to direct the rhythm, the melody, the instrumentation and other musical characteristics to compose a musical composition. 43

LOCOMOTOR MOVEMENT TO MUSIC (n = 4; 3.85%)

<u>BEHAVIOR</u>   <u>MUSIC THERAPY INTERVENTION</u>

LM-1 Participates in unstructured creative movement to music; improvises movement to music; moves creatively to music (n_1 = 2; 50.00%)

Assess the patient's spontaneous movement to music. Use patient preferred music. 35

In the presence of music, assist the clients in creating a movement pattern, then in memorizing the movement pattern. If working with a large group of clients, split the group into two or three smaller groups and have each patient take a turn performing the movement (e.g., round robin format). 43

LM-2 Dances the latest dance styles to preferred music (e.g., rap music; the latest teen-age "sensation") (n1 = 1; 25.00%)

Use the above dances to promote therapeutic goals (e.g., exercise, group leadership through demonstrating or teaching others to dance, self-expressiveness, group cohesiveness, and peer acceptance). 45

LM-3 Has trouble dancing because of the inability to respond to cues (n1 = 1; 25.00%)

Assist the client in establishing a dance routine with which she can be successful (e.g., four to six individual movements). Have the client repeat the routine to the count of eight. 36

CODE: N = Number of music therapy interventions submitted for Adolescents.

n = Number of music therapy interventions submitted for the area of assessment. % = Percentage of N.

n1 = Number of music therapy interventions submitted for the specific music behavior. % = Percentage of n1.

The number(s) after each intervention (e.g., 36) refers to the mean **Global Assessment of Functioning Scale** (*GAF Scale*) (*DSM-III-R*, 1987) score of clients for whom the intervention was designed. One score was given by each music therapist specifying the intervention (e.g., "25-30-36" indicates the particular intervention was submitted by three music therapists, and that the intervention is used with clients having the three indicated GAF scores).

PSYCHIATRIC MUSIC THERAPY ASSESSMENTS AND TREATMENTS EMPLOYED IN NAMT-APPROVED CLINICAL TRAINING FACILITIES
CHILDHOOD: MUSIC BEHAVIOR
(N = 57; 100%)

ASSESSMENT AREA

LISTENING TO MUSIC (n = 14; 24.56%)

BEHAVIOR   MUSIC THERAPY INTERVENTION

L-1   Demonstrates the ability to identify characteristics of music, such as musical style, which instruments are playing, the tempo of the music (i.e., slow or fast), and whether the selection is an instrumental or vocal; recognizes a variety of musical styles; listens discriminatively to music (n_1 = 8; 57.14%)

During music listening, have the patient identify the name of the musical selection, the style of music, the instrumentation, whether the tempo is slow or fast, whether the dynamics are loud or soft, whether the selection is an instrumental or vocal. If the selection was a vocal ask the client whether a man or woman was singing. Adjust the task to the capability of the patient. 20-20-36-40

After listening to each musical selection, ask the patient to state whether or not they liked the musical style and why. 36

Play "Instrument Bingo." This game is played the same as the usual game of Bingo with the exception that the "calls" are short excerpts of certain instruments playing. The child is asked to place a chip on the corresponding picture of the instrument that is playing (Note: Sounds of instruments may be obtained from the recording, "A Young Person's Guide to the Orchestra," Opus 32 [Britten, 1946]. Also recordings of common instruments such as piano, guitar, autoharp, and percussion instruments may be used). 40

Teach the client to identify the names of music instruments. Present flash cards to the client each with a picture of a music instrument and the name of the music instrument. Teach the client to pronounce and spell by rote the name of the music instrument. Monitor the client's correct responses. 50

Teach the client to identify instruments by family grouping, emphasizing the distinguishing characteristics of each family of instruments. 50

L-2   Demonstrates the ability to choose preferred music, or to state musical preferences ($n1 = 2$; 14.29%)

Play a variety of music and ask the client to rate the songs in order of preference. Provide assistance when needed. 40

Given a variety of record albums, the client will choose a song for music listening. 20

L-3   Reads the lyrics to songs ($n1 = 2$; 14.29%)

Give the clients a copy of the lyrics to a song. Observe the ability of the clients to read the lyrics; provide assistance if needed. 50

Give the clients a copy of the lyrics to a song. Observe the ability of the clients to follow the lyrics as the song is playing. After the song ends, conduct a discussion of the content of the lyrics and of the client's interpretation of the lyrics. 50

L-4   Identifies popular songs ($n1 = 1$; 7.14%)

Play the game, "Name That Tune." 40

L-5   Demonstrates audience behavior appropriate to a variety of live music ($n1 = 1$; 7.14%)

Take students on periodic field trips to attend live informal music performances (i.e., jazz; pop concert; street music; dance music). 20

SINGING ($n = 14$; 24.56%)

BEHAVIOR   MUSIC THERAPY INTERVENTION

S-1   Sings on pitch; matches pitch; sings in tune ($n1 = 4$; 28.57%)

Observe the client singing various childrens' songs. 86

Before singing a song, the therapist sings the first pitch of the song and the patient matches the pitch. 40

Observe the client singing acappella, a song of choice. 40

Ask the client to sing a familiar song. The therapist chooses the song to be sung and provides an instrumental accompaniment using the piano or guitar. 40

S-2   Sings melodic phrases; sings lyrics to songs (n1 = 4; 28.57%)

Sing several melodic phrases for the client. After each phrase, ask the client to sing an imitation or duplication of the phrase. 51

Teach the patient a song one line at a time by rote (the therapist sings a line, then the patient imitates). 36

Ask the patient to spontaneously sing a solo as a special feature during group singing. 56

The therapist models phrase by phrase the correct articulation of the song lyrics. After each phrase, the clients repeat the lyrics back to the therapist. This exercise is done without singing, with the rhythmic character of a chant. Body rhythms or rhythm instruments may be utilized to accompany the recitations. Following this exercise, teach the clients to sing the lyrics with the correct inflection, pitch, and intonation. Use the same technique as above with the exception that the clients sing each phrase after it is modeled by the therapist. 50

S-3   Sings with music therapist from a song book (n1 = 2; 14.29%)

Have the client choose from a song book a familiar song to sing. The therapist and the client will then sing the song together. Note the client's ability to begin and end the song on time, and the ability to maintain the tempo. 33

When discussing familiar songs, observe the child's emotional response. Does the child exhibit facial expressions such as sadness or joy? 33

S-4   Sings from the beginning to the end of a song without being distracted (n1 = 1; 7.14%)

Ask the client to perform in the center of the group as the "guest singer." Observe the client's ability to sing without becoming distracted. 56

S-5   Sings loudly enough to be heard by an audience (n1 = 1; 7.14%)

Prepare the clients to sing in a music show. During rehearsals, tape record the clients singing the music for the music show, then have them sing along with the tape recording. Challenge the clients to sing as loud as the tape recording. 56

S-6   Chooses songs from song book that are reminiscent of family members (n1 = 1; 7.14%)

During group discussion ask the children to select a song that reminds them of their family members. Read with the children the song titles in the table of contents. Observe each child's response to the song title topics. Does the child avoid or retreat from songs that remind her of various family members? 33

| S-7 | Sings a song from memory (n1 = 1; 7.14%) |

Ask the client to sing a familiar song from memory. The therapist may sing along with the client. Observe the content and mood of the song the client chooses. 33

PLAYING INSTRUMENTS (n = 11; 19.30%)

| BEHAVIOR | MUSIC THERAPY INTERVENTION |

| P-1 | Responds rhythmically to music; responds to music by keeping a rhythmic pulse (n1 = 2; 18.18%) |

During rhythm band group, have each client play a rhythm that coincides with a rhythm performed by another client. 56

During music listening, ask the student to clap her hands, nod her head, and/or tap her foot in response to a variety of musical selections and tempi. 20

| P-2 | Plays a variety of instruments (n1 = 2; 18.18%) |

Give the client the opportunity to play a variety of instruments, such as bar (Orff) instruments, guitar or autoharp, recorder, electronic keyboard, and the drum machine. 40

Have each child play a variety of Orff instruments in a pentatonic ensemble. 36

| P-3 | Plays instrument on cue; follows musical cues (n1 = 1; 9.09%) |

Ask the client to play a rhythm instrument to a song at pre-specified times as indicated by the therapist's cue. Observe the client's ability to start and stop playing on cue. 40

| P-4 | Plays autoharp; uses a class room instrument to accompany a musical selection (n1 = 1; 9.09%) |

Invite the client to participate with the music therapist in playing the autoharp (e.g., the therapist presses the chords and sings as the client strums the strings). Continue to teach basic skills necessary for playing the autoharp independently. Observe the client's memory ability, attention span, the ability to follow directions, and rhythmic ability. 33

P-5   Plays choir chimes (n1 = 1; 9.09%)

Instruct the client in the correct usage of choir chimes (e.g., holding and ringing the choir chimes). To reinforce correct usage, have the clients play from charts (choir chime music) of preferred songs. NOTE: For an example of choir chime or hand bell music, see Rubin (1976). 50

P-6   Plays guitar (n1 = 1; 9.09%)

Using nontraditional Multichord guitar technique (Cassity, 1977), play a blues progression in which each client strums their guitar upon cue. 36

P-7   Uses rhythm/lumi sticks correctly (n1 = 1; 9.09%)

Instruct the client in the correct usage of rhythm/lumi sticks. Use call and response activities to give the client experience in the correct usage of the sticks. 50

P-8   Listens to tape recording of own instrumental performance (n1 = 1; 9.09%)

Tape record the group's instrumental performance, then have the group listen to the tape following the performance. 36

P-9   Plays music instrument for peer or staff member (n1 = 1; 9.09%)

Ask the child to choose a favorite staff person with whom to share her newly acquired autoharp performance skills. Assess the child's relationship with authority figures in terms of which staff is chosen, and how she responds to the staff person. 33

LOCOMOTOR MOVEMENT TO MUSIC (n = 8; 14.04%)

BEHAVIOR   MUSIC THERAPY INTERVENTION

LM-1 Creates movements to music; performs unstructured creative movement (n1 = 2; 25.00%)

Play music that has a danceable rhythm or a clearly defined beat. Ask the patient to create a movement to the music. Observe the degree of expressiveness exhibited while moving to the music. 36-40

LM-2 Participates in choreography (n1 = 1; 12.50%)

Teach the client the steps to a choreographed movement. Note the ability of the client to remember the dance sequence. Proceed from easy to more difficult choreography. 40

LM-3 Imitates or mirrors musical movement (n1 = 1; 12.50%)

Play music of a danceable quality. Ask the patient to imitate the musical movement of the therapist or a peer. 36

LM-4 Moves in rhythm to the music; follows directions for movement (n1 = 1; 12.50%)

Observe the ability of the children to perform body action songs. For example, play the song, "Sally the Swinging Snake" and encourage the children to move to the music and to do the actions described in the song. 40

LM-5 Moves freely and spontaneously without rigidity (n1 = 1; 12.50%)

If the client exhibits rigidity in movement, start by involving the client in marching exercises. Prepare the client to eventually participate in creative movement depicting environment objects such as animals. 56

LM-6 Follows sequence of movement activity (n1 = 1; 12.50%)

If the client has difficulty following the sequence of a movement activity, involve the client in number games in which each child must respond when her number is sung (e.g., Have the clients relate numbers to objects while singing songs such as "Ten Little Pennies (Indians)," "This Old Man," and "Three Little Speckled Frogs." [Cassity, 1985]). 56

LM-7 Walks to the beat of the music (n1 = 1; 12.50%)

Ask the clients to walk in a circle to the beat of a drum. Vary the tempo of the beat and observe whether the clients alter their walking pace to match the tempo of the drum beat. 36

COMPOSING MUSIC (n = 4; 7.02%)

BEHAVIOR   MUSIC THERAPY INTERVENTION

C-1   Composes new lyrics to songs; composes a parody; participates in lyric substitution activities (n_1 = 3; 75.00%)

Give the patient experience at composing lyrics to fit the established melodic and rhythmic limits of a song. 33

Using a song which has a topic the child considers to be nonthreatening, observe the child's ability to suggest lyrics that fit rhythmically into the song phrases. Also note the complexity of words the child chooses and the accuracy of their meaning. 33

Using a song which has a topic relating to the child's problems, observe the child's ability to suggest lyrics that fit rhythmically into the song phrases. Note the child's level of insight into her problems and her assessment of the situation. 33

C-2   Composes a greeting song (n_1 = 1; 25.00%)

Have each client decide how many beats their name is. For example, Mar-ga-ret would be three beats. Next ask each client to choose an Orff instrument on which to play each beat of their name. Give each client their choice of three instruments. Next write each client's name, their chosen instrument, and the rhythmic and melodic notation of their name on an adapted music staff. Finally have the group sing a standard greeting song, with each group member playing their name at the appropriate time (e.g., Hel-lo Margaret, Hel-lo Margaret, Hel-lo Margaret, we're glad you're here today [to the tune of "Good Night Ladies"]). 36

IMPROVISING MUSIC (n = 2; 3.51%)

BEHAVIOR   MUSIC THERAPY INTERVENTION

I-1   Uses improvisation to create a song (n_1 = 1; 50.00%)

Give the patient experience at setting limits necessary to create a song. Assist the client in creating a song by improvising with instruments, body percussion, or their voice. 36

I-2	Directs the performance of an improvised song (n1 = 1; 50.00%)

After creating a song have the patient conduct the song, directing when each instrument will play and what instrument will play. 36

NON-LOCOMOTOR MOVEMENT TO MUSIC (n = 4; 7.02%)

BEHAVIOR   MUSIC THERAPY INTERVENTION

NL-1 Claps rhythms; remembers and reproduces rhythms accurately (n1 = 4; 100%)

Ask the patients to take turns mirroring each other's rhythmic clapping. 86

Clap several rhythms for the client. After each rhythm is clapped, ask the client to clap an imitation or duplication of the rhythm. 51

Play the game, "Telephone." This game is played by first dividing the children into pairs so that each child has a partner. Each child will "transmit a message" to her partner by tapping the rhythmic sequence of the message on her partner's back. The partner will acknowledge the message by repeating the tapped rhythm on the child's back. The partner is then given one minute to guess what the message was. The child may assist her partner by only using gestures or nonverbal communication. Words are not allowed. If the partner cannot guess the message within one minute the child and the partner lose a point. The partners with the most points win. 40

CODE: N = Number of music therapy interventions submitted for Childhood.

n = Number of music therapy interventions submitted for the area of assessment. % = Percentage of N.

n1 = Number of music therapy interventions submitted for the specific music behavior. % = Percentage of n1.

The number(s) after each intervention (e.g., 36) refers to the mean **Global Assessment of Functioning Scale** (*GAF Scale*) (*DSM-III-R*, 1987) score of clients for whom the intervention was designed. One score was given by each music therapist specifying the intervention (e.g., "25-30-36" indicates the particular intervention was submitted by three music therapists, and that the intervention is used with clients having the three indicated GAF scores).

Appendix I
About This Manual

Origin of Data

This manual contains patient problems and music behavior music therapists assess and treat most frequently in clinical training facilities. The information was collected from a national survey of all NAMT-approved psychiatric clinical training facilities. Clinical training directors (CTDs) submitted 801 music therapy interventions for assessing and treating 200 patient problems, and 354 interventions for assessing music behavior. This manual reports the patient problems, music behaviors, and music therapy interventions according to the frequency with which they were reportedly used in clinical training facilities. For a summary and statistical analysis of information contained in this manual the reader is referred to the *Journal of Music Therapy* (Cassity & Cassity, 1994).

In brief, clinical training directors were given areas of nonmusic behavior that had been extracted from the music therapy literature and asked to choose the areas they assess and treat most frequently during music therapy sessions. Next they were asked to write for each area they selected, two patient problems they assess and treat most frequently. Finally, for each of the patient problems they listed, they were requested to list two music therapy interventions they use most frequently to assess or treat the patient problems. A similar procedure was used to collect information about the assessment of music behavior and activity therapy assessment.

The patient problems and music therapy interventions in this manual are indexed by chronological age (CA) and level of functioning. Sex is an additional index with Adults. The CA levels are Adulthood, Adolescence, and Childhood. Infancy was not included because an insufficient number of CTDs worked with infants. Level of functioning indices were obtained by asking CTDs to rate their patients using the Global Assessment of Functioning Scale (GAF Scale) as found in the *Diagnostic and Statistical Manual of Mental Disorders III-R* (DSM-III-R) (APA, 1987).

The GAF Scale ranges from *1*, representing the most severe symptoms, to *90*, representing the mildest symptoms. The GAF is arranged into nine ten-point intervals, with each interval containing a verbal descriptor of typical patient symptoms. CTDs were asked to indicate, using the GAF Scale, the level of functioning typical of the majority of patients treated in their clinical training program. The numbers following each music therapy intervention in this manual are GAF Scale scores. Each number, or score indicates the level of functioning of the patients with whom the CTD used the intervention. For interventions having more than one GAF Scale score, the number of GAF Scale scores listed equals the number of times the intervention was submitted by different CTDs. For example, 30-40-35 indicates the intervention was submitted by three CTDs, and that the intervention was used with patients having GAF Scale scores of 30, 40, and 35. With adult patients, the GAF Scale scores are preceded by the letter *M* (Male) or *F* (Female), indicating the sex of the patient for whom the intervention was designed.

Data also were collected on the mean GAF of patients for whom this manual is designed. The mean GAF rating of adult patients was 36.5 with a median of 33. Seventy percent of the CTDs indicated the GAF level of their adult patients to be between 21 and 40. The following description applies to patients with a GAF rating of 31-40, therefore approximating the typical adult treated in psychiatric music therapy clinical training programs:

> Some impairment in reality testing or communication (e.g., speech is at times illogical, obscure, or irrelevant) or major impairment in several areas, such as work or school, family relations, judgment, thinking, or mood (e.g., depressed man avoids friends, neglects family, and is unable to work; child frequently beats up younger children, is defiant at home, and is failing at school) (APA, 1987, p. 12).

CTDs gave somewhat higher GAF ratings to their adolescent than to their adult patients. When asked to indicate, using the GAF, the level of functioning typical of the majority of adolescents treated in their clinical training program, 87% of the CTDs indicated the level of their adolescents to be between 31 and 50. The mean GAF rating was 40.5 and the median was 41. The level of functioning of the typical adolescent treated in psychiatric music therapy clinical training programs therefore would border between the above descriptor and the following for patients with a GAF of 41 to 50:

> Serious symptoms (e.g., flat affect and circumstantial speech, occasional panic attacks) OR moderate difficulty in social, occupational, or school functioning (e.g., no friends, unable to keep a job) (APA, 1987, p. 12).

Children were given the highest GAF ratings. Although 71% of all children were given GAF ratings of between 33 and 50, the mean GAF was 45.76 and the median was 45. The above descriptor therefore would approximate patients treated in psychiatric music therapy clinical training programs who were in the CA level of childhood.

Evolution of the Model

During the questionnaire analysis difficulties emerged relating to certain assessment areas and music conditions CTDs had chosen. Table A on the following page illustrates the original areas CTDs chose for adult male and female patients, and the number and percentage of CTDs choosing the areas.

Certain assessment areas in Table A, which had been extracted from the music therapy literature, and which had been chosen most frequently by music therapists were lacking in specificity. These assessment areas therefore, did not adequately define the type of problem they were to assess. An example was the assessment area, Coping. Although approximately 55% (female and male combined data) of the CTD's indicated they assessed Coping, the specific problems for Coping could have been classified within a variety of assessment areas. Thirty-two percent of the problems listed under Coping were Affective problems, 21% were Interpersonal-Socialization problems, and 29% were Cognitive problems. The highest inter-therapist agreement as to the meaning of Coping therefore, was 32%. Coping as an assessment area was too general and did not adequately refer to a specific area of assessment.

TABLE A
AREAS ASSESSED MOST FREQUENTLY IN PSYCHIATRIC CLINICAL TRAINING FACILITIES

ASSESSMENT AREA (ADULT FEMALE PATIENTS, N = 41)	n	%
AFFECT	31	75.61
SOCIALIZATION	26	63.42
COPING SKILLS	22	53.66
INTERPERSONAL	19	46.34
LEISURE SKILLS	15	36.59
COMMUNICATION	13	31.71
BEHAVIOR	12	29.27
SUBSTANCE USE OR ABUSE	11	26.83
COGNITIVE	7	17.07
PSYCHOLOGICAL	7	17.07

ASSESSMENT AREA (ADULT MALE PATIENTS, N = 35)	n	%
AFFECT	26	74.29
SOCIALIZATION	22	62.86
LEISURE SKILLS	20	57.14
COPING	20	57.14
INTERPERSONAL	18	51.43
COMMUNICATION	15	42.86
BEHAVIOR	10	28.57
COGNITIVE	8	22.86
PSYCHOLOGICAL	7	20.00
MENTAL FUNCTIONING	5	14.29
SUBSTANCE USE OR ABUSE	5	14.29
SENSORY INTEGRATIVE FUNCTIONING	3	8.57
IMAGERY	2	5.71
PHYSICAL WELL BEING	2	5.71

(Inter-therapist agreement was used in this study as an index for quantifying the degree of meaningfullness to CTDs of a given assessment area. Inter-therapist agreement used in this sense refers to the percentage of CTDs who described the same type of problem for a given assessment area. Examples are illustrated above, and in the following text).

Similar "catch-all" assessment areas that had to be discarded were Mental Functioning and Psychological with respective inter-therapist agreements of 53% and 50%. The assessment area of Communication was another example of an assessment category with low inter-therapist agreement. When CTD's wrote specific problems for Communication, 48% were Interpersonal-Socialization problems (e.g., does not verbally interact with others), and 25% were Affective problems such as the inability to identify or express emotion. Other problems and music conditions written for Communication were physical speech problems. Communication therefore, was restricted to physical speech problems since the areas of Interpersonal-Socialization (85% inter-therapist agreement) and Affect (84% inter-therapist agreement) already existed for classifying interpersonal and affective problems. The problems and music conditions which had been written for the nonspecific areas discussed above therefore, were reclassified into already existing assessment areas having the highest inter-therapist agreement and to which they were related. Affective problems, for example, were classified under Affect.

Because of the similarity of the types of problems written for the areas of Interpersonal and Socialization, these areas were combined. Because of the close relationship of Leisure Skills to Interpersonal-Socialization, and because of the 85% inter-therapist agreement as to the meaning of Leisure Skills, Leisure Skills was classified as a separate area within Interpersonal-Socialization.

Selecting a Model. Because of the above inadequacies of existing assessment areas extracted from the music therapy literature, the need emerged for a systematic therapeutic model for classifying the patient problems and interventions submitted by CTDs. A model into which all patient problems could be classified was the Multimodal Therapy model (Lazarus, 1976; 1989). In addition, the Multimodal model previously had been recommended for use in music therapy (Adleman, 1985), and used as a model for music therapy practice (Cassity & Theobold, 1990).

The Multimodal model involves comprehensive assessment and intervention across a person's BASIC ID (or basic identity). We, at base, are biochemical and neurophysiological beings. "Our personalities are the products of our ongoing BEHAVIORS, AFFECTIVE PROCESSES, SENSATIONS, IMAGES, COGNITIONS, INTERPERSONAL RELATIONSHIPS, AND BIOLOGICAL FUNCTIONS (Lazarus, p. 13)." All these factors forming the BASIC-ID, must be considered when assessing the total person. To form a sensible acronym, Lazarus labeled the biological modality "D" for drugs. BASIC-ID, therefore, stands for the basic identity of a person. According to Lazarus,

> The BASIC-ID represents the fundamental vectors of human personality just as ABCDEFG represents the notes in music. There are no HIJKLMNOP. Combinations of ABCDEFG (with some sharps or flats) will yield everything from "chopsticks" to Mozart. (Lazarus, 1989, p. 16).

Thus, Lazarus hypothesized that the BASIC-ID model can account for every condition a person encounters.

Description of the Model

Following are descriptions of each multimodal category with examples of clinical issues that may appropriately be addressed within each category.

The category of *Behavior* refers mainly to overt behaviors such as acts, habits, gestures, and reactions that are measurable and observable. The therapist may be concerned with behaviors that are interfering with the patient's happiness, what the patient would like to start doing, or what he or she would like to do more of, or do less of. In adult psychiatric music therapy, lack of assertiveness, lack of attention span, and poor eye contact are examples of behaviors of frequent concern to music therapists.

Affect refers to emotions, moods, or strong feelings. The therapist may be concerned with emotions the patient experiences most often, unwanted emotions, or no emotion. Affective problems are the most frequent type of problem CTDs assess with adolescents, and the second most frequent problem assessed with adults. With adolescents, for example, CTDs are most concerned with emotions such as the inability to identify or express feelings, inappropriate expression of feelings, anger or rage, stress reactions, and excessive anxiety.

Sensation refers to the five senses: seeing, hearing, touching, tasting, and smelling. The therapist may note negative sensations experienced by the patient such as tension, pain, dizziness, sweating, blushing, and "butterflies" in stomach. What the patient likes to taste, smell, hear, or see also may be of concern. Although CTDs assess and treat sensory disorders relatively infrequently, when they do treat them, the treatment usually involves the use of relaxation techniques with patients who are having problems coping with stress and tension.

Imagery may include recurring dreams; vivid memories that may be bothersome or troubling, the patient's self image or body image (how does the patient describe his or her self-image, "pictures" of the past, present, and future that may be troubling, and "auditory images" such as tunes or sounds heard repeatedly that are a problem. Although imagery is another infrequent assessment area in music therapy, when it is assessed it is usually during guided imagery or relaxation. The music therapist may be concerned with whether the patient can envision and focus on a pleasant place during guided imagery or relaxation. With battered women, imagery is assessed because of its importance at promoting ventilation, relaxation, and the alleviation of anxiety during relaxation and guided imagery sessions (Cassity & Theobold, 1990).

Cognitive refers to ideas, values, opinions, and attitudes that interfere with the patient's happiness. The therapist may be concerned with the patient's negative self-statements, irrational ideas (What are the patient's shoulds, oughts, and musts?), and the patient's cherished beliefs and values. Cognitive problems are the third most frequent type of problem CTDs assess with adults and adolescents, and a second most frequent problem assessed with children. With adult patients, music therapists most frequently are concerned with cognitive problems such as low self esteem as evidenced by negative self statements, deficit problem solving skills, lack of reality orientation, poor short or long term memory skills, and poor decision-making skills.

Interpersonal includes problems the patient has with other people and concerns they have about the way they are treated by others. In psychiatric music therapy, Interpersonal-Socialization is the most frequent area assessed with adults and children, and the second most frequent area of assessment with adolescents. With adult patients CTDs most frequently are concerned with reclusive, withdrawn, or isolative behavior, inappropriate use of leisure time, uncooperative behavior, a lack of interest in or lack of motivation to use leisure time, and difficulty bonding with others.

Drugs refers to any concerns the patient has about his or her state of health, or the physical well being of the patient. Such concerns could relate to the patient's habits pertaining to diet, exercise, and fitness. In addition, Drugs could refer to medications or drugs taken by the patient, substance abuse, and to drug side effects. In psychiatric music therapy, Drugs is the fourth most frequent area of assessment with adults and adolescents, and the second most frequent area of assessment with children. The assessment of Drugs with children most frequently focuses on physical well being, such as gross and fine motor coordination, and physical communication problems, such as impaired ability to describe objects, feelings or situations.

Multimodal therapy is very eclectic. It does not adhere to just one mode of therapy such as Gestalt therapy or Behavior therapy, but rather, it includes a whole gamut of therapies. The inherent eclecticism of the model makes it especially amenable for use in music therapy because of the wide diversity in music therapy practice (all chronological ages and diagnoses), and because music therapists work in settings representative of many different schools of psychotherapy. Interventions a music therapists might implement, such as relaxation training, aerobic exercises, rational-emotive therapy, and assertiveness training all could be used as treatments in a multimodal profile.

It is very important to remember that although multimodal assessment and treatment attends to specific problems, each within a given modality, it also focuses on the interaction between a given modality and the other modalities. Thus, a problem in one modality will influence problems in all other areas or modalities. This can be illustrated by the following example:

•Laura has trouble asserting herself. (Behavior)
•She feels frustrated. (Affect)
•She experiences life as being extremely stressful resulting in feelings of chronic fatigue. (Sensation)
•She fantasizes how she could "get even." (Imagery)
•She believes others are always taking advantage of her by manipulating her into doing what they would like to do instead of doing what she would like to do. (Cognitive)
•She sometimes acts in a passive-aggressive manner with her friends. (Interpersonal)
•She abuses alcohol and prescription medication to decrease feelings of fatigue. (Drugs)

Laura's not being assertive results in a whole array of problems under the BASIC-ID. We can tell a lot about what is going on in Laura's life by looking at each area.

When assessing each modality it is essential to go back and determine the effect of one area upon all the others. For example, after assessing the affect it is important to determine what the patient tends to do or how he/she behaves when feeling a certain way. For example, with a patient who is experiencing a lot of anxiety, the music therapist should say, "How do you behave when you are very anxious?" "What happens?"

Likewise, when assessing Sensory, after determining applicable sensations you go backwards and note how the sensations caused the patient to act or feel, and so on. For example, when sensations occur such as hyperventilation or muscle tension, ask the patient "How does that make you feel?" "What does that make you do?" So, as you go down the BASIC-ID you may have to go back up the BASIC-ID. Therefore, all modalities are very interdependent. By understanding the interactions among them, one is better able to achieve a thorough and holistic understanding of the person.

Functional analysis. In addition to examining the interactions among the modalities, the therapist should investigate the antecedent stimuli in a given situation, organismic or mediating variables, the subject's observable response, and the consequences. This procedure involves asking the patient *What, When, Where, Who,* and *How* questions such as the above. *Why* questions are not as productive in terms of yielding clinically relevant information (Bandler and Grinder; 1975). Asking Why questions frequently produces patient rationalization. According to Egan, the cause, especially remote causes, are seldom evident. Asking the patient to explain "...causes often is inviting them to whistle in the wind." (Egan, 1990, p. 161).

Modality firing order. Lazarus refers to modality firing order as the sequence with which the BASIC-ID modalities are exhibited during a given response pattern. Examining the interactive pattern of the modalities for purposes of determining the sequence of the firing order is referred to as *tracking.* For example, as indicated above, Laura's modality firing order was Behavior, Affect, Sensory, Imagery, Cognitive, Interpersonal, and finally, drugs. The Behavior (lack of assertiveness) produced the Affect, the Affect resulted in the Sensory, and etc. Not all modality firing orders however, follow the BASIC-ID sequence. Ron, for example had very low self esteem. He frequently made negative self statements and lacked the self confidence to try to overcome life problems or to try new activities (Cognitive). He projected his low self opinion onto others by frequently saying undesirable things about other patients and staff, resulting in peer rejection (Interpersonal). During conversation with others he had poor eye contact (Behavior). He fantasized himself as "one of the little people" and being "walked on" by others who always "come out on top." (Imagery). Following the imagery Ron recalled several sad experiences, and expressed hopelessness and pessimism about the future (Affect). Ron's modality firing order was Cognitive, Interpersonal, Behavior, Imagery, and Affect.

Affective responses or emotional disturbances therefore, can be triggered by a sequence of events. The sequence may begin with any modality (e.g., a person can dwell on thoughts and images that lead to unpleasant sensations, which may in turn lead to behavior). There is a close interaction among the various modalities. The way we feel, think, behave, etc., affects our biochemical and neurophysiological makeup, or what's going on in our body. The "Drug" modality in turn, can affect the other modalities. It is therefore important to examine the firing order, or the sequence that the modalities are exhibited during a response pattern.

Uni or bimodal interventions. At times a patient's BASIC-ID may not reveal a network of interrelated problems, or the patient may respond poorly to multifaceted intervention and insists on working on one or two problems. Although a multimodal assessment usually is recommended, the therapist and patient may choose to work on one or two clear-cut problems in such situations. If therapeutic progress is not made however, or if the patient is given an ambiguous or faltering diagnosis, a multimodal assessment may prove helpful.

Structural profiles. Structural profiles sometimes are constructed during the initial assessment phase. Some people may tend to be feelers, thinkers, doers, fantasizers, etc. The patient who is primarily a thinker, for example, may prefer to work on cognitive problems rather than in other modalities. Such knowledge may assist the therapist in structuring the therapeutic session to elicit greater involvement from the patient. The process of treating problems within a patient's preferred modality before delving into more clinically relevant problems within less preferred modalities is referred to as *bridging.*

Lazarus (1989) uses the *Structural Profile Inventory* to determine the structural profile of patients. The *Structural Profile Inventory* provides information on the extent to which patients operate in the various modalities. The Profile consists of 35 statements, each related to a given modality within the BASIC-ID. The patient rates each item on a scale of from 1 (Strongly Disagree) to 7 (Strongly Agree). Profile results can then be analyzed graphically, usually using a histogram, to indicate the extent that the patient is functioning in each modality.

The patient, therapist, or both may draw up a structural profile. If the patient is assigned to do their own structural profile it is recommended they be provided with a written description of each modality area in the BASIC-ID as given above.

Group therapy. According to Lazarus, multimodal therapy may be conducted as group therapy. Lonely, isolated individuals who need the opportunity to make friends benefit considerably from group therapy. Multimodal group therapy may be especially appropriate for music therapy since a major music therapy goal is the development of interpersonal relationships. Poor candidates for group therapy are patients who are severely depressed, paranoid, delusional, or who have ritualistic obsessive compulsive characteristics.

Lazarus recommends certain procedures and principles of group therapy. During the first session, patients are helped to feel more at ease if a discussion is conducted about the benefits of group therapy. During the second session patients are helped to construct their own modality profiles. The remainder of the sessions are devoted to working on each patient's problems as specified in her modality profile. After the group members become experienced with multimodal therapy, they usually derive benefit from tracking their modality firing order. Finally, Lazarus recommends that group therapy sessions be time limited. If groups are told that therapy will be concluded for example, after 25 sessions, the group usually achieves more.

Second-order BASIC-ID.[S] A Second-order BASIC-ID is sometimes contructed when therapeutic progress falters because of a persistent patient problem within a given modality. For example in the above case of Laura, therapeutic goals may be to increase assertiveness, decrease feelings of frustration, and so on, down her

BASIC-ID. If however, therapeutic progress falters because of her increasing alcohol abuse, a second-order BASIC-ID may need to be constructed to focus exclusively on her alcohol abuse:

B. Drinks excessively at local bar and at home.
A. Expriences depression as a result of drinking.
S. Has migrain headaches as a result of alcohol abuse.
I. Imagines she is in total control of her drinking; fantasizes her bar life as glamerous.
C. Denies having a drinking problem.
I. Increasing interpersonal problems are the fault of others (e.g., inconsiderate boss); associates with bar crowd.
D. Alcohol abuse has dramatically increased.

Finally, it should be emphasized that Lazarus has documented impressive outcomes and follow-ups using the multimodal approach to assessment and treatment. Possibly by using this systematic approach in the field of psychiatric music therapy we can experience more success in the assessment and treatment of our patients.

Most Frequent Modalities in Psychiatric Music Therapy
During the initial assessment phase it may be most productive to assess first the modalities assessed most frequently by CTDs. CTDs prefer to assess and treat certain modalities significantly more frequently than others with adults ($X2 = 298.20$; $p < .001$), adolescents ($X2 = 126.27$; $p < .001$), and children ($X2 = 39.79$; $p < .001$). As indicated in Tables B, C, and D, 76% of all adult problems and 85% of all adolescent problems assessed or treated by CTDs were either Interpersonal, Affective, or Cognitive problems. With children, Interpersonal, Behavior, Cognitive, and Physical (including motor and receptive and expressive language) problems accounted for 82% of all problems assessed or treated by CTDs.

TABLE B
MODALITIES ASSESSED AND TREATED MOST FREQUENTLY
IN PSYCHIATRIC MUSIC THERAPY CLINICAL TRAINING FACILITIES:
ADULTS

MODALITY	NUMBER OF PROBLEMS ASSESSED	% OF PROBLEMS
INTERPERSONAL	177	33.27
AFFECT	121	22.37
COGNITIVE	112	20.70
BEHAVIOR	55	10.17
DRUGS	54	9.98
SENSORY	20	3.70
IMAGERY	2	00.37
	541	100.56

TABLE C
MODALITIES ASSESSED AND TREATED MOST FREQUENTLY
IN PSYCHIATRIC MUSIC THERAPY CLINICAL TRAINING FACILITIES:
ADOLESCENTS

MODALITY	NUMBER OF PROBLEMS ASSESSED	% OF PROBLEMS
AFFECT	51	32.69
INTERPERSONAL	49	31.41
COGNITIVE	32	20.51
DRUGS	12	7.69
BEHAVIOR	11	7.05
IMAGERY	1	00.64
SENSORY	0	00.00
	156	99.99

TABLE D
MODALITIES ASSESSED AND TREATED MOST FREQUENTLY
IN PSYCHIATRIC MUSIC THERAPY CLINICAL TRAINING FACILITIES:
CHILDREN

MODALITY	NUMBER OF PROBLEMS ASSESSED	% OF PROBLEMS
INTERPERSONAL	32	30.77
BEHAVIOR	18	17.31
DRUGS	18	17.31
COGNITIVE	18	17.31
AFFECT	10	9.62
SENSORY	6	5.77
IMAGERY	2	1.92
	104	100.01

Appendix II
Tutorial Guide: Use Of This Manual

Initial Assessment

During the initial assessment phase, in addition to using music to establish rapport, the patient's life history is reviewed, the patient is interviewed to determine present problems, and the *Psychiatric Music Therapy Questionnaire* is administered. This information is then used to construct the patient's multimodal profile.

Information concerning life history may be determined by reviewing assessments given by other professionals such as the social worker or psychologist. Music therapists who do not have access to assessments given by other professionals may obtain life history information by administering the *Multimodal Life History Questionnaire* (Lazarus, 1989).

After interviewing the patients about their present life situations, the *Psychiatric Music Therapy Questionnaire* is administered. There are three *Psychiatric Music Therapy Questionnaires*, one each for adults (Appendix III), adolescents (Appendix IV), and children (Appendix V). The Questionnaires for adults and adolescents are administered by interviewing the patient, and the Questionnaire for children is administered by interviewing a significant third person, such as the child's parent.

The Questionnaires are designed to provide intake information concerning problems most frequently treated using music therapy. Items in each questionnaire are indexed to specific problems addressed in this treatment manual. An example of the indexing is illustrated in the Questionnaire for adolescents on page 206 of Appendix IV. The "(A-1)" after the first item, "Other people know when I am happy, sad, or excited. (A-1)" indicates the item, and any other item following it, is a measure of the "Inability to identify/express feelings...," the first problem (A-1) listed under adolescent Affect on page vi of the Table of Contents. The Table of Contents in turn, refers the reader to page 48 under adolescent Affect in the manual, where music therapy interventions are listed for treating the "Inability to identify/express feelings...." If the music therapist decides to use one of the interventions, the intervention is written in the patient's multimodal music therapy profile.

The *Psychiatric Music Therapy Questionnaire* requires patients to rate themselves on a five-point scale, with "1" indicating "Strongly Disagree" and "5" indicating they "Strongly Agree." Generally, questionnaire items rated "4" or "5" are considered to be indicative of patient problems, and therefore should be included in the multimodal music therapy profile. An exception is with items having a reversed scale, that are stated in the positive rather than in the negative. For these items a patient rating of "1" or "2" would generally be the criterion for inclusion in the multimodal music therapy profile.

The assessment areas in the Questionnaires are not presented in the same order as in the BASIC-ID or the manual, but rather according to the frequency that they are assessed and treated by music therapists. For example, Appendix I indicated that with adolescents, music therapists most frequently assess and treat affective problems, followed by interpersonal, cognitive, etc. This order therefore, was the one used for the assessment areas in the Questionnaire for adolescents.

Following is a summary of the initial assessment procedure: (1) Review the patient's case history; (2) Administer the questionnaire that is appropriate for the patient's chronological age level; (3) Construct a BASIC-ID to get the *big picture* of the patient's problems and to compare the agreement of questionnaire results with case history results; (4) Construct a multimodal music therapy profile from the questionnaire results. Because of the unique needs of different patients, the manual should not be used as a cookbook approach to music therapy. The music therapist therefore, may choose *not* to select interventions from the manual for inclusion in the multimodal music therapy profile.

Program Planning

Once the initial assessment has been conducted, goals, objectives, and implementation strategies may be planned. The implementation strategy provides information concerning the materials needed, type of reinforcement, therapist behavior, and patient behavior. Progress is then charted and evaluated in the session/monthly progress report.

Case Example: Adults

The following case of *D* provides an example of how to derive a multimodal analysis from the initial assessment.

Case of *D*

DATE: October 13, 1993

D is a 35-year old male receiving support services at a community mental health center. According to *D,* his mother had schizophrenia, and his grandmother took responsibility for him. At age three *D* was placed in a Masonic home. During childhood *D* was sexually and physically abused from age three on, and had no church affiliation. *D* later stated that during this time he "learned to show no feelings." By age 16 *D* was drinking heavily, taking illegal street drugs, and recalled that he "had no family." At age 19 he was placed in a metropolitan crisis center. *D* never married and was rejected by the military.

Despite these difficulties *D* did garner some achievements. He graduated from high school, then attended the University of Oklahoma for three years as a Russian studies major. In Russian studies he was described as being a bright student with grades averaging a B+. During his senior year he transferred to a regional university as a psychology major. Although the WAIS-R indicated he had an IQ of 80, the quotient probably was inaccurate because of his psychosis. *D* was beginning to experience symptoms of schizophrenia. At age 22, *D* was employed as an aide at a state psychiatric hospital where he remained for 10 years. *D* reported spending his leisure time engaging in reading or "doing nothing."

When *D* was 34 he was admitted to a state hospital (different from the one where he had been employed) for treatment of schizophrenia. Several months later he was referred to a community mental health center with the goal of community placement. It was recommended that *D* first be placed in a transitional lodge, then given continuous community support services to prevent further hospital returns and episodes of active schizophrenia. At the community mental health center he was described as having poor leisure skills (no hobbies), lacking in daily living skills, having poor personal hygiene, withdrawn, severely depressed and passive. Other assessments revealed that although *D* had been a bright student, his speech (thought processes) was characterized by slowness, blocking, hesitancy, incoherence, simplicity, and concreteness. His thought content was suicidal, evidenced guilt, disturbed by recurring fantasies (which he would not discuss), and high in persecutory beliefs and hallucinatory perceptions. Immediate retention and recall were adequate, but short term and long term memory was inadequate. *D* was given the following diagnosis:

Axis I: 295.70 Schizoaffective Disorder.
           305.00 Alcohol Abuse.
Axis II: 301.84 Passive Aggressive Personality Disorder
Axis III: None
Axis IV: Psychosocial Stressor: Repeated physical sexual abuse.
           Severity: 4 – Severe
Axis V: Current GAF: 50; flat affect; moderate difficulty in social functioning.

After reviewing *D's* history and administering the *Psychiatric Music Therapy Questionnaire* for adults, the following BASIC I.D. was compiled from the case history and Questionnaire results to provide a systematic and comprehensive overview of *D's* problems.

MODALITY	PROBLEMS
Behavior	Lack of assertiveness; has difficulty expressing own views on a topic during group discussion; passive.
Affect	Feelings of anger and stress. Depressed
Sensation	Hallucinatory perceptions
Imagery	Recurring fantasies that *D* will not discuss
Cognitive	Low self esteem; low self opinion; lack of self confidence Poor short and long term memory Persecutory beliefs Suicidal thought content
Interpersonal	Reclusive, withdrawn, isolative Poor leisure skills Difficulty maintaining long term relationships
Drugs	Haldol: 10 mg. each evening; 150 mg. once a month Cogentin: 2 mg. per day Benedryl: 50 mg at night Absence of daily exercise; poor muscle tone. Substance abuse history Poor personal hygiene

Following construction of the above BASIC-ID, *D's* Multimodal Music Therapy Profile was constructed. The purpose of the multimodal profile is to target problems for music therapy intervention, and to specify the type of music therapy intervention to be used. The problems in the profile are the types of problems music therapists most commonly treat, as indicated in this manual.

Multimodal Music Therapy Profile: *D*

I. MUSIC PREFERENCES

D's favorite type of music is Jazz. He also likes rock, religious, and classical. Neutral responses were given in the areas of popular and country music. He dislikes folk music. He did not indicate a preference for a favorite performer or composer. *D* would very much like to learn to play the saxophone or guitar, and likes to participate in group sing-a-longs accompanied by a pianist or guitarist.

II. MULTIMODAL PROBLEM ANALYSIS

Interpersonal	Problem	Music Therapy Intervention
IS-1	**Reclusive, Withdrawn, Isolative.**	•Elicit patient discussion of song characteristics during music listening. •Play socialization games such as "Stop the Music." •Instrumental or improvisation group requiring nonverbal and verbal interaction with others (e.g., leading the group; listening to and responding to others).
IS-2	Poor leisure skills;	•Determine specific style(s) of jazz preferred as well as other music preferences. •Provide leisure education (e.g., community music and nonmusic activities; building a tape library). •Take on field trips to community music events.
IS-5	**Difficulty maintaining long term relationships.**	•Encourage patient bonding during above group singing and instrumental groups. •During above listening-discussion group, use songs that focus on positive aspects of relationships and friendships.
Affect	Problem	Music Therapy Intervention
A-3	**Feelings of anger and stress.**	•During above listening-discussion group, from a list of titles expressing frustration, have patient select a title that expresses his feelings. Use techniques in manual to encourage expression of source of anger.
Cognitive	Problem	Music Therapy Intervention
C-1	**Low self esteem Low self opinion Lack of self confidence**	•Engineer the above instrumental music therapy activities to produce patient feelings of success, accomplishment, and peer acceptance. •Use success oriented music activities or lessons. Ask patient to point out positive aspects of their playing.

C-5	**Poor short and long term memory involving time, place, names and events.**	•During the above group singing activity, ask the patient to identify his favorite song, the name of the song just sung, questions about song lyrics, musical characteristics (e.g., tempo, melody), etc. •Promote recognition of names of peers.
Behavior B-1	Problem **Lack of assertiveness; Has difficulty expressing own views on a topic during group discussion.**	Music Therapy Intervention •During above listening-discussion activity, have the patient identify assertive and non assertive messages in the song lyrics. •Engineer group situations in which the patient must negotiate with another patient (e.g., which song to play or sing). •Have patients list things they enjoy most then communicate them to the group (Song: "My Favorite Things").
Drugs D-1.2	Problem Check for possible denial of substance abuse problem.	Music Therapy Intervention •Use song discussion techniques for detecting denial (see manual, page 38).
D-2.1	**Absence of daily exercise; poor muscle tone.**	•Involve the patient in regular rhythmic exercise.
Medication	Haldol: 10 mg. each evening; 150 mg. once a month; Cogentin: 2 mg. per day; Benedryl: 50 mg. at night	•Observe for possible medication side effects.

III. POST INTERVIEW OBSERVATIONS

D had good concentration, attention span, and retention. He appeared to be physically out of shape, had a flat affect, and projected low self confidence and self concept. He seemed to have a favorable attitude toward participation in music therapy.

In the above multimodal analysis, the column on the left indicates the modality or area of assessment, the center column refers to the patient's problem, and the right column is the music therapy intervention used to treat the problem. Letter numbers in the left column under each area of assessment refer to the order that problems are listed under each modality in the manual, and in the Table of Contents. For example, the letter number IS-1 is written under "Interpersonal," and to the left of "Reclusive, Withdrawn, Isolative" in the above modality analysis. Page iv of the Table of Contents indicates reclusive, withdrawn, isolative is the first, or most frequent problem music therapists treat in the Interpersonal-Socialization modality, and that the problem can be found on page 26. On page 26 "Reclusive; Withdrawn; Isolative behavior" is listed and is followed by the types of music therapy interventions used most frequently to treat the problem. Likewise, the letter number A-3 under Affect in the above modality analysis refers to the third problem listed under Affect on page iii of the Table of Contents, "Becomes angry when coping with frustration." This problem is listed at the bottom of page nine and is followed by the music therapy interventions used most frequently to treat the problem.

Also in the above multimodal analysis, the problems in bold lettering were problems that *D* indicated were most severe. A perusal of the above multimodal analysis indicates a predominance of such problems. Because of the preponderance of problems which *D* rated as a "4" or "5" in the questionnaire, it was decided to focus on *D's* most severe problems. To list all the problems would have made the profile unmanageable. Also, an examination of the questionnaire results revealed that in most cases, the lesser problems were probably being exacerbated by the more severe problems. Eagan (1990) uses the term *leverage* to refer to the process of ameliorating lesser problems by targeting more severe or primary patient problems. One problem listed which was rated a "4" was "poor leisure skills." Leisure skills were targeted because of the possibility that they might directly enhance chances for improvement in the other areas targeted, by contributing to *D's* life satisfaction, self confidence, and socialization.

Another problem, "Substance Use," was included in *D's* profile even though it was rated a "3." *D* gave a neutral response to the Questionnaire statement, "I do not have a substance abuse problem." This may indicate *D* either believes he has been rehabilitated, or that he cannot admit he has a substance abuse problem (denial). Also, this statement apparently is the only questionnaire response that is inconsistent with *D's* case history and diagnosis. It was therefore decided to use music therapy to attempt to determine whether *D* was denying having a substance abuse problem.

Because *D* had many problems that are treated frequently in music therapy, and because of *D's* music preferences, *D* was accepted for music therapy. The following goal, objectives, and implementation plan are representative of the first ones constructed for *D.* The intervention and implementation plans below focus on the first music therapy intervention listed in D's Multimodal Profile (above) for his reclusive and withdrawn behavior.

MUSIC THERAPY INTERVENTION PLAN

NAME: D   CASE NO: 0001
DATE OF ASSESSMENT: 10-08-93

Music Therapy Goals and Objectives

* *

Goal #1: Interpersonal-Isolation
Goal Statement: *D* will demonstrate socialization skills by 10-94.

Objective #1.1 Objective Statement: During music listening, *D* will verbalize more than a yes or no response in discussion, when prompted by the therapist, in 4 out of 5 sessions by 1-5-94.

Person Responsible: *John Doe, RMT-BC*
Date Started: 10-09-93   Date Ended:
Reason Ended:

Objective #1.2 Objective Statement: During music listening, *D* will spontaneously verbalize more than a yes or no response in discussion of selected music, in 4 out of 5 sessions by 5-1-94.

Person Responsible: *John Doe, RMT-BC*
Date Started: 10-22-93   Date Ended:
Reason Ended:

Objective #1.3 Objective Statement: [NOTE: Record any future socialization objectives for Goal #1 here.]

Person Responsible:
Date Started: Date Ended:
Reason Ended:

Following construction of the intervention plan, implementation strategies are constructed. Following is an example of an implementation strategy.

IMPLEMENTATION STRATEGY

NAME: *D*   CASE NO: 0001
DATE OF ASSESSMENT: 10-08-93

OBJECTIVE #1.1
Materials Needed: Guitar or piano; jazz music selected by *D.*

Reinforcement Schedule: Continuous verbal reinforcement in sessions 1-10.

THERAPIST BEHAVIOR   PATIENT BEHAVIOR

•Play *D's* preferred style of jazz   •*D* attentively listens to music
                                          or *D* does not.

•Ask *D* open-ended questions to elicit   •*D* answers question or *D* does not.
participation in discussion (e.g., a
question that requires a response
other than "yes" or "no.")

During the course of treatment, the following was used to chart *D's* progress.

CUSTER COUNTY MENTAL HEALTH CENTER
Music Therapy Progress Report Chart

Patient Name____D_____Therapist Name *John Doe, RMT-BC*

Specify goal and objective being worked on in the space provided. Place the appropriate evaluation code under the session date to indicate whether or not the objective was met, if the patient was absent, or if there was insufficient time to work on the objective. Write a session/monthly progress report.

Goal #1: *D* will demonstrate socialization skills by 10-94
Objective #1.1: During music listening, D will verbalize more than a yes or no response in discussion of selected music, in 4 out of 5 sessions by 1-5-94.

Date: *October 1993*   / *10-9* / *10-16* / *10-23* / *10-30* /
Progress: -   -   +   A

EVALUATION:
Record a "+" for completion of objective.
Record a "-" for not meeting objective.
Record an "A" for patient or therapist being absent
Record an "0" for insufficient time during the session to work on the objective.

Session/Monthly Progress Report

_____
_____
_____
_____
_____
_____
_____
_____

Goal #1: *D* will demonstrate socialization skills by 10-94
Objective #1.2: During music listening, D will spontaneously verbalize more than a yes or no response in discussion of selected music, in 4 out of 5 sessions by 5-1-94.

Date: *Nov. 1993* / *11-1* / *11-7* / *11-14* / *11-21* / *11-28* /
Progress: -   -   +   A   -

EVALUATION:
Record a "+" for completion of objective.
Record a "-" for not meeting objective.
Record an "A" for patient or therapist being absent
Record an "0" for insufficient time during the session to work on the objective.

Session/Monthly Progress Report

_____
_____
_____
_____
_____
_____
_____
_____

Case Examples: Adolescence

The following case material provides examples of how to derive multimodal analyses, goals, objectives, and implementation strategies for adolescents.

Case of *M*

DATE: September 17, 1993

M is a 15-year old male adolescent presently living at a specialized community home. *M* was placed in DHS (Department of Human Services) custody December 3, 1991. Since that time he has spent approximately six weeks living at home with his family. During the rest of the time, he has resided in a variety of different settings including foster care and youth shelter.

M has not had contact with his natural father since he was five months old. His mother was married to an abusive man from 1979-1982. Both mother and child were physically abused. *M'* s abusive step father works on an oil rig and his mother is a nurse. *M* has a brother age 17, and a 12 year old sister.

The *Minnesota Multiphasic Personality Inventory* for adolescents suggests a valid profile. *M* 's pattern of evaluations on the basic clinical scales were similar to adolescents who are referred to treatment because of defiant, impulsive, and mischievous behavior. Their chief defense mechanism is acting out. They are described as assertive, hard headed, impatient, impulsive, pleasure seeking, good natured, self centered, demanding and reckless. *M* showed evidence of an overall low functioning level, a conduct disorder, and some adjustment problems connected to family stresses and the recent change in placement and schools.

M received a psychological evaluation on May 6, 1993. The *Wechsler Intelligence Scale for Children III* indicated *M* to have a verbal IQ of 76, a performance IQ of 79, and a full scale IQ of 76. An October 1991 psychological evaluation however, indicated *M* 's full scale IQ to be 91.

M is reported to have suicidal tendencies. He does not interact well in groups unless he is engaged in sports, in which case he is outspoken. He has been described as having a sociopathic personality, however, his age disqualifies him from such a diagnosis.

After reviewing *M's* case history and administering the *Psychiatric Music Therapy Questionnaire* for adolescents, the following BASIC-ID was compiled to provide an overview of *M's* problems.

MODALITY	PROBLEMS
Behavior	——
Affect	Anger or rage towards others Excessive anxiety Impulsive Difficulty sharing feelings about significant life experiences
Sensation	——
Imagery	——

Cognitive	Lacks problem solving skills Low frustration tolerance Fighting with parents; poor conflict resolution skills.
Interpersonal	Uncooperative behavior Lacks awareness of self and others (e.g., calls others derogatory names)
Drugs	——

Following construction of the above BASIC-ID, *M's* Multimodal Music Therapy Profile was constructed.

Multimodal Music Therapy Profile: *M*

I. MUSIC PREFERENCES

M's favorite type of music is rap. He also likes country and rock. Neutral responses were given in the areas of popular and jazz music. He dislikes religious music and folk music. *M's* favorite group is Criss Cross. *M* indicated he would like to learn to play the guitar.

II. MULTIMODAL PROBLEM ANALYSIS

Affect	Problem	Music Therapy Intervention
A-2	**Exhibits anger or rage towards other people.**	•Have the patient select a song from an album to express the anger being felt. Follow up by having the patient identify personal, appropriate alternatives for ventilating the anger.
A-4	Excessive anxiety.	•Progressive muscle relaxation (PMR). •Guided Imagery – Imagine anxious situations then a positive outcome; follow-up with discussion. Assign the patient to do imagery and help select appropriate music.
A-5	Impulsive.	•Use relaxation techniques such as biofeedback, music response, and key word response. •Give piano or guitar instruction to provide experience at self control.

		•Provide for positive peer experiences through music.
A-6	**Difficulty sharing feelings about significant life experiences (e.g., traumas or fears).**	•Music listening with discussion of lyrics related to patient's traumas or fears. •Establish patient trust in the therapist using song writing and improvisational activities.
<u>Interpersonal</u> IS-1	<u>Problem</u> Uncooperative Behavior.	<u>Music Therapy Intervention</u> •Involve patient in an instrumental group; assign responsibilities so each patient's cooperation is dependent upon group success; e.g., group improvisation.
IS-2	**Lacks awareness of self and others (e.g., calls others derogatory names).**	•Have the patient accompany other patients, and to take solos while being accompanied in the above group. Encourage other awareness during follow-up discussions; e.g., "I like the way *John* played."
IS-3	**Withdrawal (e.g., does not talk when in a group).**	•Encourage group involvement by utilizing activities of interest to the patient, such as music listening with graded discussion, music composition, instrumental, group singing, and musical games.
<u>Cognitive</u> C-2	<u>Problem</u> **Lacks problem solving skills.**	<u>Music Therapy Intervention</u> •Use guided imagery and music relaxation. During guided imagery ask the patient to imagine problem situations and to mentally rehearse being in control. In follow-up discussion, give patient experience at discovering successful management strategies for problems.
C-3	**Low frustration tolerance.**	•Adjust above guitar or piano lessons to insure success, with the goal of increasing frustration tolerance. •Involve the patient in additional activities such as song writing and music improvisation to reduce frustration and inappropriate behavior.

| C-8 through C-10 | **Fighting with parents; Poor conflict resolution skills.** | •Improvisation using instruments to represent family members; discuss appropriate solutions. •Discuss appropriate solutions to problem oriented song lyrics (e.g., "Cat's in the Cradle.") Generalize to patient. |

III. POST INTERVIEW IMPRESSIONS

Post interview impressions indicated a high degree of concentration, retention, and an adequate attention span. *M* exhibited appropriate facial expressions, posture, and was appropriately groomed.

The above initial assessment indicated *M* to have Affective, Interpersonal, and Cognitive problems. In addition, they are the types of problems most frequently treated by music therapists. Although additional problems may be noted later during the treatment phase, the above initial assessment provides information concerning the most important problems, and ample data for initiating a music therapy program of treatment, complete with music therapy goals and objectives. *M* therefore, was accepted for music therapy.

The intervention plans and strategies designed for *M* contain goals, behavioral objectives, procedures, and evaluation criteria. Following is an example of an intervention plan for helping *M* to appropriately express his anger.

MUSIC THERAPY INTERVENTION PLAN

NAME: *M*   CASE NO: 0002
DATE OF ASSESSMENT: 10-02-93

Music Therapy Goals and Objectives

* *

Goal #1: Affect-Anger
Goal Statement: *M* will learn appropriate methods of expressing anger by 1-2-94.

Objective #1.1 Objective Statement: During music listening *M* will select songs expressing anger to which he relates in 4 out of 5 sessions by 12-01-93.

Person Responsible: *John Doe, RMT-BC*
Date Started: 10-09-93   Date Ended:
Reason Ended:

Objective #1.2 Objective Statement: In discussions that follow music listening, *M* will verbalize 5 personal, appropriate alternatives for ventilating his anger in 4 out of 5 sessions by 1-2-94.

Person Responsible: *John Doe, RMT-BC*
Date Started: 10-9-93   Date Ended:
Reason Ended:

Objective # 1.3 Objective Statement: (NOTE: Write any additional objectives for Goal #1 here)

Person Responsible:
Date Started: Date Ended:
Reason Ended:

Following construction of the intervention plan, the implementation strategy is constructed. Following is an example of an implementation strategy constructed for *M*.

IMPLEMENTATION STRATEGY

NAME: *M*   CASE NO: 0002
DATE OF ASSESSMENT: 10-02-93

OBJECTIVE #1.1
Materials Needed: Guitar or piano; psychiatric song or lyric book.

Reinforcement Schedule: Continuous verbal reinforcement in sessions 1-10.

THERAPIST BEHAVIOR	PATIENT BEHAVIOR
•Prompt *M* to select a song that describes his feelings.	•*M* selects a song or *M* does not.
•Play the song for *M*.	
•Ask *M* why he chose the song.	•*M* gives reason or *M* does not.
•Ask *M*, "What feelings does the song describe?"	•*M* describes feelings in song or M does not.
•Follow in discussion.	
•If *M* does not select a song expressing his anger, repeat the above procedure except ask him to select a song expressing his anger.	

Following the construction of the Implementation Strategy, music therapy sessions were initiated and the following chart was used to record *M's* progress.

CUSTER COUNTY MENTAL HEALTH CENTER
Music Therapy Progress Report Chart

Patient Name____*M*____Therapist Name *John Doe, RMT-BC*

Specify goal and objective being worked on in the space provided. Place the appropriate evaluation code under the session date to indicate whether or not the objective was met, if the patient was absent, or if there was insufficient time to work on the objective. Write a session/monthly progress report.

Goal #1: *M* will learn appropriate methods of expressing anger by 12-16-93.
Objective #1.1: During music listening M will select songs expressing anger to which he relates in 4 out of 5 sessions by 12-01-93.

Date: *October 1993*   / *10-9* / *10-16* / *10-23* / *10-30* /
Progress: A   -   +   -

EVALUATION:
Record a "+" for completion of objective.
Record a "-" for not meeting objective.
Record an "A" for patient or therapist being absent
Record an "0" for insufficient time during the session to work on the objective.

Session/Monthly Progress Report

_____

_____

_____

_____

_____

_____

_____

Goal #1: *M* will learn appropriate methods of expressing anger by 12-16-93.
Objective #1.2: In discussions that follow music listening, *M* will verbalize 5 personal, appropriate alternatives for ventilating his anger in 4 out of 5 sessions by 1-2-94.

Date: *October 1993*   / *10-9* / *10-16* / *10-23* / *10-30* /
Progress: A   -   -   +

EVALUATION:
Record a "+" for completion of objective.
Record a "-" for not meeting objective.
Record an "A" for patient or therapist being absent
Record an "0" for insufficient time during the session to work on the objective.

Session/Monthly Progress Report

_____
_____
_____
_____
_____
_____
_____
_____
_____

The case of *B* is provided as a further example of how to construct a multimodal music therapy profile with adolescents.

Case of *B*

Date: September 24, 1993

B is a 16-year old male adolescent presently living at a specialized community home. *B* was placed in DHS custody May 15, 1991. Since that time *B* has resided in a variety of different settings including foster care and youth shelter.

B's biological father is reported to be in prison. *B* was made aware of his identity a year and a half ago, but has never met him. *B's* mother was using drugs at the time of his birth, and his great grandparents requested and received custodial care of him at three months. His natural mother and step father him visit sporadically. Contact with siblings is minimal and inconsistent.

B was born chemically dependent. At age three, *B* was diagnosed as being hyperactive and placed on Ritalin. He continued this medication until he was in kindergarten.

B received a psychological evaluation in 1991. The *Wechsler Intelligence Scale-Revised* indicated *B* to have a verbal IQ of 80, a performance IQ of 101, and a full scale IQ of 89. His strength was his ability to organize and remember visually perceived material as well as visual motor coordination. Weaknesses included verbal comprehension, difficulty with concentration, and a tendency to be distractive. The *Bender Gestalt* indicated developmental lags, and immature mental and emotional development. Feelings of inferiority and the tendency to withdraw from others were revealed, along with hostile feelings of a covert nature. Projective drawings indicated emotional impulsive desires to repress thoughts and memories with an almost childlike avoidance of reality. *B* makes attempts at controlling his emotions but few resources render him successful.

After reviewing *B's* case history and administering the *Psychiatric Music Therapy Questionnaire* for adolescents, the following BASIC – I.D. was compiled.

MODALITY	PROBLEMS
Behavior	Mediocre attention span and concentration Inadequate eye contact
Affect	Excessive anxiety Difficulty relating life experiences to others Observe for signs of emotional imaturity
Sensation	——
Imagery	——
Cognitive	Weakness in verbal comprehension. Feelings of inferiority
Interpersonal	Withdrawn Does not engage in leisure activities May lack knowledge of leisure activities
Drugs	——

Following construction of the above BASIC-ID, *B's* Multimodal Music Therapy Profile was constructed.

Multimodal Music Therapy Profile: *B*

I. MUSIC PREFERENCES

B stated he likes country, popular, rock, and religious music equally. He is neutral about jazz and dislikes folk music. *B's* favorite group is Alice in Chains. *B* expressed a desire to participate in a music listening group.

II. MULTIMODAL PROBLEM ANALYSIS

Affect	Problem	Music Therapy Intervention
A-4	Excessive anxiety.	•Progressive muscle relaxation. •Guided imagery – imagine anxious situations then a positive outcome; discuss. Assign the patient to do imagery and assist in selecting appropriate music.
A-6	Difficulty relating life experiences to others.	•Establish patient trust in the music therapist. Use song writing, improvisation, and song lyric discussion related to the patient's fears or traumas.

Interpersonal	Problem	Music Therapy Intervention
IS-3	Withdrawal.	•Encourage group involvement by utilizing activities of interest to the patient, such as music listening with graded discussion, music composition, instrumental, group singing, and musical games.
IS-4 through IS-5	May lack knowledge of leisure activities. Does not engage in leisure activities.	•Give music lessons; encourage home practice. •Consider patient involvement in music groups such as school or community band, orchestra, chorus, church choir, and popular music ensemble. •Expose patient to arts entertainment and activities in the community.

Behavior	Problem	Music Therapy Intervention
B-2	Mediocre attention span and concentration.	•Adjust involvement in music lessons to accommodate attention span (e.g., length of lesson and practice time; five minute breaks during practice time; gradually longer playing times).

Not specified	Inadequate eye contact.	•Gradually encourage more and more eye contact from the patient during the above music therapy activities. Require the patient to watch for musical cues.

III. POST INTERVIEW OBSERVATIONS

Post interview impressions indicate a mediocre degree of concentration, retention, and attention span. *B* exhibited appropriate facial expressions and posture, and was groomed properly. Eye contact appeared to be inadequate.

     B 's profile indicates eye contact as a problem. Although eye contact is not listed in the manual under Adolescents, it was listed as a problem in *B* 's profile because of his inadequate eye contact during the initial interview.

     The above initial assessment indicated *B* to have affective, interpersonal, and behavioral problems. Other problems across the BASIC-ID may emerge during treatment, especially if the music therapist decides to perform a second order BASIC-ID as described in Appendix I. The above profile however, provides ample justification and information for the initiation of music therapy with *B*. The decision therefore, was to accept *B* for music therapy.

Case Example: Children
Following is an example of an initial assessment with *J.*

Case of *J*

Date: September 22, 1993

J is a six year old female who has been receiving treatment at a community mental health center since July 29, 1993. *J* 's mother and father have been divorced for 18 months, and were separated for four years before the divorce. *J's* mother has since remarried. *J* has a sister age four, and an 18 month old brother. *J* is presently living at home with her mother and step-father. *J* 's biological father who is homosexual and living with another man, sees *J* every other week.

In kindergarten *J* is learning slowly and has difficulty recalling concepts. *J* likes to read books, listen to music, and play with dolls in her spare time. *J* 's mother reported that *J* frequently wets the bed. *J* frequently states "I want to be myself; nobody loves me." *J* was thought to be autistic at an earlier age. She was reported to engage in seductive behavior and sexual play that could be the result of over stimulation through overexposure to sexual material. No definite incidence of sexual abuse was noted.

During *J* 's personal interview she was very talkative and engaged in a great deal of story telling. During the interview she exhibited an unusual tremor in the upper part of her body. Despite the unusual body movements and apparent learning difficulties, *J* appeared intelligent in some areas. No physical developmental delays were noted.

J's problems were not interacting well with peers, learning problems, poor emotional expression, and unprovoked violent, angry behavior. Her strengths were that her mother and step-father are supportive, she is enrolled in kindergarten, and her mother adequately takes care of her needs. *J* was referred for a neurological examination and admitted to group therapy, with individual therapy provided as needed. *J* 's mother was referred to outpatient therapy. *J* was given the following diagnosis:

Axis I: 309.28 Adjustment Disorder With Mixed Emotional Features.
            V61.20 Parent-Child Problem.
Axis II: 315.90 Specific Developmental Disorder NOS.
Axis III: None
Axis IV: Psychosocial stressors: Separation and divorce of parents; remarriage of
            mother.
            Severity: 3 – Moderate.
Axis V: Current GAF: 50

After interviewing *J's* mother, observing *J,* reading the assessments of other professionals, and administering the *Psychiatric Music Therapy Questionnaire* for children to *J's* mother, the following BASIC-ID was constructed for *J.*

MODALITY	PROBLEMS
Behavior	Unassertive; does not express needs Off task; easily distracted; poor concentration; short attention span Hits peers Poor eye contact
Affect	Has trouble describing how others feel Exhibits too many emotional extremes
Sensation	
Imagery	
Cognitive	Difficulty following directions Makes negative self statements; low self esteem; lacks self confidence to participate in group activities Poor method and quality of approach to tasks Makes derogatory comments to peers if they don't do what she wants

Interpersonal	Does not follow rules and regulations
	Makes negative comments to peers (i.e., name calling)
	Minimal or no verbal interaction with peers
	Is not attentive in structured activities (e.g., does not pay attention to others)
	Poor leadership skills
Drugs	Poor speech articulation
	Poor comprehension

Following construction of the above BASIC-ID, *J's* Multimodal Music Therapy Profile was constructed.

Multimodal Music Therapy Profile: *J*

I. MUSIC PREFERENCES

J's mother stated *J* strongly prefers popular, children's, folk, religious, new age, and classical music. She likes country music and is neutral about rock music. Her favorite recording is Kitaro (New Age).

II. MULTIMODAL PROBLEM ANALYSIS

Interpersonal	Problem	Music Therapy Intervention
IS-1	Does not follow rules and regulations.	•Use contingent music techniques.
IS-1	Makes negative comments to peers (i.e., name calling).	•Use contingent music techniques.
IS-2	Minimal or no verbal interaction with peers.	•Use a rhythm band to encourage nonverbal peer interaction. •Music listening techniques in which patient chooses songs for peer, or that describes peer. •Encourage interaction in a variety of "fun" music activities.
IS-5	Is not attentive in structured activities (e.g., does not pay attention to others)	•During a pentatonic instrumental ensemble, use eye contact to cue or communicate when each individual is to start or stop playing her instrument. Reinforce on task behavior.

IS-7	Poor leadership skills.	•Assign the patient leadership roles during the above rhythm instrument activity (e.g., Display STOP and GO signs to signal when the group starts or stops playing).
Behavior	**Problem**	**Music Therapy Intervention**
B-1	Unassertive; does not express needs.	•Have patient conduct above instrumental groups with a baton communicating dynamics, tempo, starting and stopping. •Elicit nonverbal and verbal choice of instrument. •Play musical games that require the patient to ask questions.
B-2	**Off task; easily distracted; poor concentration; short attention span.**	•Reinforce in seat behavior using instrumental play activities. •Have patient sing while maintaining a rhythmic beat; use gradually longer songs.
B-4	Hits peers.	•Involve the patient in a puppet show focused on a musical drama about feelings. •Contingent music.
B-5	**Poor eye contact.**	•Elicit eye contact by singing the child's name in a song. •Have patient give and receive performance cues using eye contact in above instrumental activities.
Drugs (Motor)	**Problem**	**Music Therapy Intervention**
D-2.4	Poor speech articulation.	•Emphasize clear pronunciation while singing songs and chanting the lyrics. Review speech pathology assessment.
D-2.5	Poor comprehension.	•Discuss the meaning of song lyrics during the above singing activities.
Cognitive	**Problem**	**Music Therapy Intervention**
C-1	**Difficulty following directions.**	•Assign tasks during above instrumental activities (e.g., playing an ostinato rhythmic pattern). •Give directions during above singing activities (e.g., finding page numbers). •Use body action songs and simple dances requiring the following of one-step, two-step, and multi-step directions.

C-3	**Makes negative self statements; low self esteem; Lacks self confidence to participate in group activities.**	•Record number of positive self and peer statements as patient assesses musical accomplishments. •Increase self confidence through successful group participation (e.g., above instrumental groups; games such as "Music Charades.").
C-4	Poor method and quality of approach to tasks.	•Instrumental performance activities (e.g., using the autoharp to provide a chordal accompaniment to a song; playing an ostinato pattern on the marimba.)
C-5	Makes derogatory comments to peers if they don't do what she wants.	•During song writing, teach the sharing of concepts by singing the children's thoughts, feelings, and ides about appropriate ways of meeting one's needs.
<u>Affect</u> A-1	<u>Problem</u> Has trouble describing how others feel; Exhibits too many emotional extremes.	<u>Music Therapy Intervention</u> Teach patient to describe and to appropriately express feelings. (e.g., see "feeling card" activity, instrumental, and song techniques in the manual).

III. POST INTERVIEW OBSERVATIONS

J exhibited poor eye contact, limited concentration, and short attention span.
Interpersonal relationships appeared mediocre. She seems very interested in music.

J's Questionnaire results indicated deficits in telling time, counting money, memorizing the letters of the alphabet, and counting. Although these deficits were rated a "5" in the questionnaire, they were not given top priority in J's music therapy plan. Because of the developmental level of the patient (CA = 6) and the severity of J's emotional problems, top priority was assigned to treating the emotional problems. Plans were made however, to meet with J's teacher to discuss academic goals.

Because J had a multitude of the types of problems music therapists commonly treat, J was accepted for music therapy. Following is J's Music Therapy Intervention Plan for improving her ability to follow directions.

MUSIC THERAPY INTERVENTION PLAN

NAME: *J*   CASE NO: 0004
DATE OF ASSESSMENT: 9-22-93

Music Therapy Goals and Objectives

* *

Goal #1: Cognitive-Following Directions
Goal Statement: *J* will follow directions in group activities by 10-22-93.

Objective #1.1: Objective Statement: During an instrumental activity, *J* will play her instrument when her instrument and name are mentioned in a song selected by the therapist, 4 out of 5 times correctly.

Person Responsible: *Jane Doe, RMT-BC*
Date Started: 10-1-93   Date Ended:
Reason Ended:

Objective #1.2: Objective Statement: During group activity, *J* will verbally select a song that the person sitting next to her might enjoy, one song per session, for one consecutive month.

Person Responsible: *Jane Doe, RMT-BC*
Date Started: 10-1-93   Date Ended:
Reason Ended

Objective # 1.3: Objective Statement: (NOTE: Write any additional objectives for Goal #1 here)
Person Responsible:
Date Started: Date Ended:
Reason Ended:

Following is *J's* implementation strategy for improving her ability to follow directions.

IMPLEMENTATION STRATEGY

NAME: *J*   CASE NO: 0004
DATE OF ASSESSMENT: 9-22-93

OBJECTIVE #1.1
Materials Needed: Rhythm instruments, guitar, or piano.

Reinforcement Schedule: Contingent music; continuous positive reinforcement.

THERAPIST BEHAVIOR	PATIENT BEHAVIOR
•Ask all the children to join hands with each other (to form a circle). •Seat the children "Indian style" and give each child a rhythm instrument.	•Child joins hands or child does not. •Child sits on the floor or child does not. •Child appropriately accepts or rejects rhythm instrument or child inappropriately accepts or rejects rhythm instrument.* (*If child makes a negative comment while being handed her instrument, tell the child that is not the appropriate way to disagree; assist the child in appropriately disagreeing. Either do not give the child an instrument and explain why, or give the child an instrument if the child makes a satisfactory disagreement.)
•Explain to the children that you (the therapist) are going to sing a song and in the song their names and their instruments are mentioned. When they hear their instrument and name they play until another instrument starts. Explain to the children that if they play out of turn they will be asked to sit out one turn in the song.	•Child plays when her name and name of instrument are sung or child does not.

The following chart was used to record *J's* progress.

CUSTER COUNTY MENTAL HEALTH CENTER
Music Therapy Progress Report Chart

Patient Name_____J_____Therapist Name *Jane Doe, RMT-BC*

Specify goal and objective being worked on in the space provided. Place the appropriate evaluation code under the session date to indicate whether or not the objective was met, if the patient was absent, or if there was insufficient time to work on the objective. Write a session/monthly progress report.

Goal #1: *J* will follow directions in group activities by 10-22-93.
Objective #1.1: During an instrumental activity, *J* will play her instrument when her instrument and name are mentioned in a song selected by the therapist, 4 out of 5 times correctly by 10-22-93.

Date: *Oct. 1993* / *10-1* / *10-7*   / *10-14* / *10-21* / *10-28* /
Progress: -   -   +   A   +

EVALUATION:
Record a "+" for completion of objective.
Record a "-" for not meeting objective.
Record an "A" for patient or therapist being absent
Record an "0" for insufficient time during the session to work on the objective.

Session/Monthly Progress Report

_____
_____
_____
_____
_____
_____
_____
_____

```
┌─────────────────────────────────────────────────────────────────────┐
│ Goal #1: J will follow directions in group activities by            │
│ 10-22-93.                                                            │
│ Objective #1.2: During group activity, J will verbally select a song│
│ that the person sitting next to her might enjoy, one song per session,│
│ for one consecutive month by 10-22-93.                              │
│                                                                      │
│ Date: Oct. 1993 / 10-1 / 10-7    / 10-14 / 10-21 / 10-28 /          │
│ Progress:          -      -        +       +       +                 │
│                                                                      │
│ EVALUATION:                                                          │
│ Record a "+" for completion of objective.                           │
│ Record a "-" for not meeting objective.                             │
│ Record an "A" for patient or therapist being absent                 │
│ Record an "0" for insufficient time during the session to work on the objective. │
│                                                                      │
│                   Session/Monthly  Progress  Report                  │
│                                                                      │
│ _____ │
│ _____ │
│ _____ │
│ _____ │
│ _____ │
│ _____ │
│ _____ │
│ _____ │
│ _____ │
└─────────────────────────────────────────────────────────────────────┘
```

Practice Exercises

Following are some case histories to provide practice in the construction of modality profiles, intervention plans, implementation strategies, and charting progress. Read each case history, complete a *Psychiatric Music Therapy Questionnaire* the way you think the patient would complete it, construct a BASIC-ID, then construct a modality profile based on the Questionnaire results and the case history. After constructing the music therapy modality profile, write an intervention plan, an implementation strategy, and chart hypothetical progress.

CASE STUDY I, ADULTS: SICKLY*

A 38-year-old married woman came to a mental health clinic with the chief complaint of depression. In the last month she had been feeling depressed suffering from insomnia, frequently wept, and had been aware of poor concentration and diminished interest in activities.

The patient relates that she was sickly as a child and has been depressed since childhood because her father deserted the family when she was approximately ten. Apparently she was taken to the doctor for this and the family doctor recommended that her mother give the patient a little wine before each meal. Her adolescence was unremarkable although she describes herself as having been shot. She graduated from high school at age 17 and began working as a clerk and bookkeeper at a local department store. She married at about the same age, but the marriage was not a success: She had frequent arguments with her husband, in part related to her sexual indifference and pain during intercourse.

At age 19 she began to drink heavily, with binges and morning shakes which she would relieve by having a drink as soon as she got up in the morning. She felt guilty that she was not caring adequately for her children because of her drinking. At 21 she was admitted to a local mental hospital where she was diagnosed as suffering from alcoholism and depression. She was treated with antidepressants. After discharge she kept drinking almost continually; when she was 29, she was again hospitalized this time on the alcohol treatment unit. Since then she has remained abstinate. She has subsequently been admitted to psychiatric hospitals for a mixture of physical and depressive symptoms, and once was treated with a course of electroconvulsive therapy, which produced little relief.

The patient describes nervousness since childhood; she also spontaneously admits being sickly since her youth with a succession of physical problems doctors often indicated were due to her nerves or depression. She, however, believes that she has a physical problem that has not yet been discovered by the doctors. Besides nervousness, she has chest pains, and has been told by a variety of medical consultants that she has a "nervous heart." She often goes to doctors for abdominal pain and has been diagnosed as having a "spastic colon." She has seen chiropractors and osteopaths for backaches, for pain in the extremities, and for anesthesia of her finger tips. Three months ago, she experienced vomiting, chest pain, and abdominal pain, and was admitted to a hospital for a hysterectomy. Since the hysterectomy she has had repeated anxiety attacks, fainting spells that she claims are associated with unconsciousness that last for more than 30 minutes, vomiting, food intolerance, weakness, and fatigue. She has had surgery for an abscess of the throat.

The patient is one of five children. She was reared by her mother after her father left. Her father was said to have been an alcoholic, he died at age 53 of liver cancer. Despite a difficult childhood financially, the patient graduated from high school and worked two years. She tried to work a second time, but was forced to quit because of her sickliness. Her husband is said to be an alcoholic who has had some periods of work instability. They have argued about sex and finances. They have five children, ranging in age from 2 to 20.

*Taken from Spitzer, R. L., Gibbon, M., Skodol, A. E., Williams, J. B. W., and First, M. B. (1989). *DSM-III-R Case Book.* Washington, D. C.: American Psychiatric Press, Inc., pp. 90–93.

The patient currently admits to feeling depressed, but thinks it is all because her "hormones were not straightened out." She is still looking for a medical explanation for her physical and psychological problems.

DSM-III-R   Diagnosis:

Axis I: 296.31 Major Depression, Recurrent, Mild (p. 222)
               300.81 Somatization Disorder (Provisional) (p. 263)
               303.90 Alcohol Dependence, in Remission (p. 167)
Axis II: 799.90 Diagnosis deferred
Axis III: Vomiting, fainting
Axis IV: Psychosocial Stressors: recent hysterectomy
               Severity: 4-Severe (predominantly acute event)
Axis V: Current GAF: 50
               Highest GAF past year: 50

Complete a *Psychiatric Music Therapy Questionnaire* for adults the way you think SICKLY would complete it, then construct a BASIC-ID for SICKLY based on the case history and the Questionnaire results.

MODALITY	PROBLEMS
Behavior	
Affect	
Sensation	
Imagery	
Cognitive	

Interpersonal
_____
_____
_____

Drugs
_____
_____
_____
_____

Following completion of the above BASIC-ID, refer to the
Questionnaire results to construct a Multimodal Music Therapy
Profile.

Multimodal Music Therapy Profile: _____

I. MUSIC PREFERENCES

_____
_____
_____
_____

II. MULTIMODAL PROBLEM ANALYSIS

Interpersonal	Problem	Music Therapy Intervention
____	_____	_____
____	_____	_____
____	_____	_____
____	_____	_____
____	_____	_____
____	_____	_____

Affect	Problem	Music Therapy Intervention
____	_____	_____
____	_____	_____
____	_____	_____
____	_____	_____
____	_____	_____

Cognitive	Problem	Music Therapy Intervention
_____	_____	_____
_____	_____	_____
_____	_____	_____
_____	_____	_____
_____	_____	_____
_____	_____	_____

Behavior	Problem	Music Therapy Intervention
_____	_____	_____
_____	_____	_____
_____	_____	_____
_____	_____	_____
_____	_____	_____
_____	_____	_____

III. POST INTERVIEW OBSERVATIONS

_____
_____
_____
_____
_____
_____

Assuming SICKLY was accepted for music therapy, write a Music Therapy Intervention Plan.

MUSIC THERAPY INTERVENTION PLAN

NAME: _____   CASE NO: _____

DATE OF ASSESSMENT _____

Music Therapy Goals and Objectives

* *

Goal #1: _____
Goal Statement: _____

Objective #1.1: Objective Statement: _____
_____
Person Responsible: _____
Date Started: _____   Date Ended: _____
Reason Ended: _____
_____

Objective #1.2: Objective Statement: _____
_____
_____
Person Responsible: _____
Date Started: _____   Date Ended: _____
Reason Ended: _____
_____
Objective #1.3: Objective Statement: _____
_____
_____
Person Responsible: _____
Date Started: _____   Date Ended: _____
Reason Ended: _____
_____

Next write an Implementation Strategy for SICKLY.

IMPLEMENTATION STRATEGY

NAME: _____   CASE NO: _____

DATE OF ASSESSMENT _____

OBJECTIVE #1.1
Materials Needed:_____

Reinforcement Schedule:_____

THERAPIST BEHAVIOR   PATIENT BEHAVIOR

_____   _____
_____   _____
_____   _____
_____   _____
_____   _____
_____   _____
_____   _____
_____   _____
_____   _____
_____   _____
_____   _____
_____   _____
_____   _____
_____   _____
_____   _____
_____   _____

Name of Agency _____
              Music Therapy Progress Report Chart

Patient Name_____ Therapist Name _____

Specify goal and objective being worked on in the space provided.
Place the appropriate evaluation code under the session date to
indicate whether or not the objective was met, if the patient was
absent, or if there was insufficient time to work on the
objective.Write a session/monthly progress report.

Goal #1: _____
_____ .
Objective #1.1:_____
_____
_____

Date: /   /   /   /   /   /
Progress:

EVALUATION:
Record a "+" for completion of objective.
Record a "-" for not meeting objective.
Record an "A" for patient or therapist being absent
Record an "0" for insufficient time during the session to work on the objective.

Session/Monthly Progress Report

_____
_____
_____
_____
_____
_____
_____
_____

Goal #1: _____

_____ .

Objective #1.2:_____

_____

_____

Date: /   /   /   /   /   /

Progress:

EVALUATION:
Record a "+" for completion of objective.
Record a "-" for not meeting objective.
Record an "A" for patient or therapist being absent
Record an "0" for insufficient time during the session to work on the objective.

Session/Monthly Progress Report

_____

_____

_____

_____

_____

_____

_____

_____

CASE STUDY II, ADULTS: HUNGARIAN OPERA SINGER*

Eva, a 39-year-old Hungarian opera singer, is re-admitted to a psychiatric hospital after keeping her family awake for several nights with a prayer and song marathon. She is flamboyantly dressed in a floor-length red skirt peasant blouse, and is adorned with heavy earrings, numerous necklaces and bracelets, and medals pinned to her bosom. She speaks very rapidly and is difficult to interrupt as she talks about her intimate relationship with God. She often breaks into song, explaining that her beautiful singing voice is a special gift that God has given her to compensate for her insanity. She uses it to share the joy she feels with others who are less fortunate.

Eva has had a least 10 admissions to this hospital in the past 20 years, some because of serious suicide attempts she made when she was depressed, some because she was manic, and some, in her words, "just because I was crazy." Although she does have a lovely voice, she has not been able to organize herself to work professionally during the past 15 years, and has spent much of her time at the local community mental health center. She has seen the same therapist weekly for many years, and believes that he communicates through a local radio station, giving her instructions on how to conduct her life between therapy sessions. She also receives illuminations from Kahlil Gibrean and Adele Davis, whose conversations she is able to overhear.

Follow-up: Eva has been hospitalized many times in the seven years following the admission described here. She has been treated with an antipsychotic drug, Haloperidol, and a mood stabilizer, lithium; but her psychotic symptoms and her extreme mood swings have been poorly controlled. She is often agitated, yelling and screaming nonstop and referring to bizarre delusions and hallucinations of "voices saying crude things about people's genitals." Most of the time she is psychotic but neither manic nor depressed.

Eva was living with her mother and her son. As her son became an adolescent his resentment of her behavior led him to taunt and provoke her. Eva's mother found it increasingly difficult to maintain the peace as she became older. After Eva's last hospital admission, she refused to take her daughter back which necessitated transferring Eva to a state hospital. The state hospital refused to keep her for more than a few weeks; when last contacted she was again creating havoc in her mother's home.

DSM-III-R   Diagnosis:

Axis I: 295.70 Schizoaffective Disorder, Bipolar Type
Axis II: 799.90 Deferred
Axis III: V71.09 None
Axis IV: Inadequate information
Axis V: GAF = 25

---

*Taken from Spitzer, R. L., Gibbon, M., Skodol, A. E., Williams, J. B. W., and First, M. B. (1989). *DSM-III-R Case Book.* Washington, D. C.: American Psychiatric Press, Inc., pp. 210–212.

Complete a *Psychiatric Music Therapy Questionnaire* for adults the way you think HUNGARIAN OPERA SINGER would complete it, then construct a BASIC-ID for HUNGARIAN OPERA SINGER based on the case history and the Questionnaire results.

MODALITY   PROBLEMS

Behavior

_____
_____
_____

Affect

_____
_____
_____

Sensation

_____
_____
_____

Imagery

_____
_____
_____

Cognitive

_____
_____
_____

Interpersonal

_____
_____
_____

Drugs

_____
_____
_____

Following completion of the above BASIC-ID, refer to the Questionnaire results to construct a Multimodal Music Therapy Profile.

Multimodal Music Therapy Profile: _____

I. MUSIC PREFERENCES

_____
_____
_____
_____

II. MULTIMODAL PROBLEM ANALYSIS

Interpersonal	Problem	Music Therapy Intervention
____	_____	_____
____	_____	_____
____	_____	_____
____	_____	_____
____	_____	_____
____	_____	_____

Affect	Problem	Music Therapy Intervention
____	_____	_____
____	_____	_____
____	_____	_____
____	_____	_____
____	_____	_____
____	_____	_____

Cognitive	Problem	Music Therapy Intervention
____	_____	_____
____	_____	_____
____	_____	_____
____	_____	_____
____	_____	_____
____	_____	_____

Behavior	Problem	Music Therapy Intervention
____	_____	_____
____	_____	_____
____	_____	_____
____	_____	_____
____	_____	_____

III. POST INTERVIEW OBSERVATIONS

_____
_____
_____
_____
_____

Assuming HUNGARIAN OPERA SINGER was accepted for music therapy, write a Music Therapy Intervention Plan.

MUSIC THERAPY INTERVENTION PLAN

NAME: _____   CASE NO: _____

DATE OF ASSESSMENT _____

Music Therapy Goals and Objectives

* *

Goal #1: _____
Goal Statement:_____

Objective #1.1: Objective Statement: _____
_____
_____
Person Responsible: _____
Date Started: _____   Date Ended: _____
Reason Ended: _____
_____
Objective #1.2 : Objective Statement:_____
_____
_____
Person Responsible: _____
Date Started: _____   Date Ended: _____
Reason Ended: _____
_____
Objective #1.3 : Objective Statement:_____
_____
_____
Person Responsible: _____
Date Started: _____   Date Ended: _____
Reason Ended: _____
_____

Next write an Implementation Strategy for HUNGARIAN OPERA SINGER then hypothetically chart her progress.

IMPLEMENTATION STRATEGY

NAME: _____   CASE NO: _____

DATE OF ASSESSMENT _____

<u>OBJECTIVE #1.1</u>
Materials Needed:_____

Reinforcement Schedule:_____

THERAPIST BEHAVIOR   PATIENT BEHAVIOR

_____   _____
_____   _____
_____   _____
_____   _____
_____   _____
_____   _____
_____   _____
_____   _____
_____   _____
_____   _____
_____   _____
_____   _____
_____   _____
_____   _____
_____   _____
_____   _____
_____   _____
_____   _____
_____   _____
_____   _____
_____   _____
_____   _____
_____   _____
_____   _____
_____   _____
_____   _____
_____   _____
_____   _____
_____   _____
_____   _____
_____   _____

Name of Agency _____

Music Therapy Progress Report Chart

Patient Name_____ Therapist Name _____

Specify goal and objective being worked on in the space provided. Place the appropriate evaluation code under the session date to indicate whether or not the objective was met, if the patient was absent, or if there was insufficient time to work on the objective. Write a session/monthly progress report.

Goal #1: _____
_____ .
Objective #1.1:_____
_____
_____

Date: /   /   /   /   /   /
Progress:

EVALUATION:
Record a "+" for completion of objective.
Record a "-" for not meeting objective.
Record an "A" for patient or therapist being absent
Record an "0" for insufficient time during the session to work on the objective.

Session/Monthly Progress Report

Goal #1: _____

_____ .

Objective #1.2:_____

_____

_____

Date: /   /   /   /   /   /

Progress:

EVALUATION:
Record a "+" for completion of objective.
Record a "-" for not meeting objective.
Record an "A" for patient or therapist being absent
Record an "0" for insufficient time during the session to work on the objective.

Session/Monthly Progress Report

CASE STUDY III, CHILDHOOD: NO ONE HITS THE BABY*

Four-year-old Carol was referred for an evaluation when her teacher made a complaint to the state Central Registry for Child Abuse Reports. A family evaluation by a social worker revealed the following:

Carol is the older of two children, both of whom live with their parents in a two-bedroom apartment. her problems began with the birth of her sister three months ago. Her teachers noticed a change in her behavior at school. She began pushing other children and hit a classmate with a wooden block, causing a laceration of the classmate's lip. When Carol's teacher took her aside to talk about her behavior, she noticed what seemed to be belt marks on Carol's abdomen and forehead.

Carol's sister was "colicky" and slept for only short periods throughout the day and night. She stopped crying only when her mother held her. Her mother therefore had little time for Carol, and Carol's father took over her care on evenings and weekends. He began to drink more than usual, half a bottle of wine each evening, and became increasingly irritable. He and his wife argued over her attention to the infant and the requirement that he take care of Carol. Carol, who was a bright, curious, talkative four-year-old, asked constant questions and often wanted to hold the baby. When refused, she would lie on the floor and have a tantrum. Since her sister's birth, she had begun to have difficulty falling asleep, and awoke repeatedly during the night. Carol's father was unable to cope with her demands for attention and often told her to shut up and slapped her when she did not obey. On many occasions he responded to her tantrums or repeated questions by hitting her with his belt.

Carol is a lively and attractive little blue-eyed blond, dressed in jeans, T-shirt, and sneakers. She relates appropriately and warmly to the interviewer and easily separates from her parents in the waiting room. Her intelligence appears above average, as indicated by her fund of knowledge, vocabulary, and drawings of a person and of geometric forms. About her sister, Carol says, "She's a bad girl. She cries all the time. I get hit when I cry, but no one hits the baby." When asked about fights at the day-care center, she replies, "I hit Robert (her playmate) because he pulls my hair." She says she is afraid to go to sleep because she has bad dreams of an old man killing her.

DSM-III-R Diagnosis:

Axis I: 309.40 Adjustment Disorder with Mixed Disturbance of
           Emotions and Conduct (p. 330)
Axis II: None
Axis III: None
Axis IV: Psychosocial Stressor: Physical abuse
           Severity: 5 – Extreme (Predominantly acute events)
Axis V: Current GAF: 55
           Highest GAF: 85

---

*Taken from Spitzer, R. L., Gibbon, M., Skodol, A. E., Williams, J. B. W., and
   First, M. B. (1989). *DSM-III-R Case Book.* Washington, D. C.: American
   Psychiatric Press, Inc., pp. 346–347.

Complete a *Psychiatric Music Therapy Questionnaire* for childhood the way you think Carol's mother or teacher would complete it, then construct a BASIC-ID for Carol based on the case history and the Questionnaire results.

MODALITY	PROBLEMS
Behavior	
Affect	
Sensation	
Imagery	
Cognitive	
Interpersonal	
Drugs	

Following completion of the above BASIC-ID, refer to the Questionnaire results to construct a Multimodal Music Therapy Profile.

Multimodal Music Therapy Profile: _____

I. MUSIC PREFERENCES

_____
_____
_____
_____

II. MULTIMODAL PROBLEM ANALYSIS

Interpersonal	Problem	Music Therapy Intervention
____	_____	_____
____	_____	_____
____	_____	_____
____	_____	_____
____	_____	_____
____	_____	_____

Behavior	Problem	Music Therapy Intervention
____	_____	_____
____	_____	_____
____	_____	_____
____	_____	_____
____	_____	_____

Drugs	Problem	Music Therapy Intervention
____	_____	_____
____	_____	_____
____	_____	_____
____	_____	_____
____	_____	_____

Cognitive	Problem	Music Therapy Intervention
____	_____	_____
____	_____	_____
____	_____	_____
____	_____	_____

Affect	Problem	Music Therapy Intervention
____	_____	_____
____	_____	_____
____	_____	_____
____	_____	_____

III. POST INTERVIEW OBSERVATIONS

_____

_____

_____

_____

_____

Assuming Carol was accepted for music therapy, write a Music Therapy Intervention Plan.

MUSIC THERAPY INTERVENTION PLAN

NAME: _____   CASE NO: _____

DATE OF ASSESSMENT _____

Music Therapy Goals and Objectives

* *

Goal #1: _____
Goal Statement: _____

Objective #1.1: Objective Statement: _____

_____

_____

Person Responsible: _____
Date Started: _____   Date Ended: _____
Reason Ended: _____

_____

Objective #1.2: Objective Statement: _____

_____

_____

Person Responsible: _____
Date Started: _____   Date Ended: _____
Reason Ended: _____

_____

Objective #1.3: Objective Statement: _____

_____

_____

Person Responsible: _____
Date Started: _____   Date Ended: _____
Reason Ended: _____

_____

Next write an Implementation Strategy for Carol, then hypothetically chart her progress.

IMPLEMENTATION STRATEGY

NAME: _____   CASE NO: _____

DATE OF ASSESSMENT _____

OBJECTIVE #1.1
Materials Needed:_____

Reinforcement Schedule:_____

THERAPIST BEHAVIOR   PATIENT BEHAVIOR

Name of Agency _____
                Music Therapy Progress Report Chart

Patient Name_____ Therapist Name _____

Specify goal and objective being worked on in the space provided.
Place the appropriate evaluation code under the session date to
indicate whether or not the objective was met, if the patient was
absent, or if there was insufficient time to work on the objective.
Write a session/monthly progress report.

| Goal #1: _____ |
| _____ . |
| Objective #1.1:_____ |
| _____ |
| _____ |

Date: /   /   /   /   /   /
Progress:

EVALUATION:
Record a "+" for completion of objective.
Record a "-" for not meeting objective.
Record an "A" for patient or therapist being absent
Record an "0" for insufficient time during the session to work on the objective.

Session/Monthly Progress Report

_____
_____
_____
_____
_____
_____
_____
_____

Goal #1: _____

_____ .

Objective #1.2:_____

_____

_____

Date: /   /   /   /   /   /
Progress:

EVALUATION:
Record a "+" for completion of objective.
Record a "-" for not meeting objective.
Record an "A" for patient or therapist being absent
Record an "0" for insufficient time during the session to work on the objective.

Session/Monthly Progress Report

_____

_____

_____

_____

_____

_____

_____

_____

_____

Appendix III

Psychiatric Music Therapy Questionnaire: Adults

PATIENT IDENTIFICATION FORM

NAME _____ SEX _____ AGE _____

FORMAL/PRIMARY DIAGNOSIS:

AXIS I:_____

AXIS II:_____

AXIS III:_____

AXIS IV:_____

AXIS V: Current GAF: _____ Highest GAF past year: _____

TOTAL NUMBER AND LENGTH OF STAYS OF PRIOR HOSPITALIZATIONS:

HOSPITAL	LENGTH OF STAY
_____	_____
_____	_____
_____	_____

LENGTH OF HOSPITALIZATION AT PRESENT FACILITY _____

TYPES OF MEDICATION TAKEN *AND*	DOSAGE PRESCRIBED
_____	_____
_____	_____

PSYCHIATRIC MUSIC THERAPY QUESTIONNAIRE
ADULTS

INSTRUCTIONS: Parts I and II of the following questionnaire are to be administered by the <u>examiner, or therapist, interviewing the examinee, or patient.</u> Part III, Post Interview Observations, will be completed by the examiner following termination of the interview, or Part II.
EXAMINER: A major purpose of therapy is to assist you with problems that may be interfering with your ability to enjoy life to the fullest. The purpose of this questionnaire therefore, is to assist you in recognizing problems or "bad habits" you may have and wish to get rid of. Since these questions are personal, you may be assured of complete confidentiality. NO ONE WILL SEE YOUR ANSWERS OTHER THAN THE THERAPISTS. If you do not care to answer these questions simply tell me you do not care to answer these questions.

I. MUSIC (viii)

1. EXAMINER: For the following styles of music tell me the number that indicates the degree you like each type of music (Examiner gives the attached scale, like the one below, to the examinee.). (viii)

	Strongly Dislike	Dislike	Neutral	Like	Strongly Like
COUNTRY	1	2	3	4	5
POPULAR	1	2	3	4	5
ROCK	1	2	3	4	5
JAZZ	1	2	3	4	5
FOLK	1	2	3	4	5
RELIGIOUS	1	2	3	4	5
OTHER _____	1	2	3	4	5

2. EXAMINER: Who is your favorite performer or composer?

(INSTRUCTION: Examiner writes in name below)

_____.

INSTRUCTIONS FOR EXAMINER: Give the examinee the scale, like the one below, attached to this questionnaire. The examinee may then refer to the scale as necessary when choosing a number.

EXAMINER: I am going to read some statements. After each statement tell me the number from this scale that describes the extent you agree with the statement.

Strongly Disagree	Disagree	Neutral	Agree	Strongly Agree
1	2	3	4	5

3. _____ I would like to participate in a group sing-a-long with a pianist or guitarist accompanying the group. (ix)

4. _____ I would like to sing on stage before an audience.

5. _____ I would like to learn to play a music instrument.

II. MULTIMODAL PROBLEM ANALYSIS

INSTRUCTIONS FOR EXAMINER: Let the examinee continue to keep the scale, like the one below. The examinee may then refer to the scale as necessary when choosing a number.

EXAMINER: I am going to read some statements. After each statement tell me the number from this scale that describes the extent you agree with the statement.

Strongly Disagree 1	Disagree 2	Neutral 3	Agree 4	Strongly Agree 5

Interpersonal (iv)

1. _____ I would rather be alone than be with people. (IS-1)
2. _____ I find it hard to make friends.
3. _____ I have no close friends.
4. _____ It is easy for me to talk to people
5. _____ It is hard for me to talk when in a group of people.
6. _____ I have trouble listening to others when they talk to me.
7. _____ I do not have a hobby; I rarely do something just for fun. (IS-2, IS-4)
8. _____ I would rather be alone or do nothing than to do something for fun with other people.
9. _____ There is not much to do in my spare time other than to sleep or watch television.
10. _____ I often get into trouble for not following directions, rules or regulations, or for not doing what I am suppose to do (e.g., smoking, eating, or drinking where prohibited). (IS-3)
11. _____ Friendships or relationships with other people usually do not last more than one year. (IS-5)
12. _____ I fight a lot with either my spouse (husband or wife) or family.
13. _____ I would feel very uneasy telling a group of people my likes, dislikes, and personal experiences. (IS-6)

14. _____ I have no difficulty being accepted by community groups (e.g., church; service groups) and with being invited to their events (e.g., parties; "get togethers;"). (IS-7)

15. _____ I would rather sit behind the group members or sit alone than to sit with the group. (IS-8)

16. _____ I say the right things when trying to make friends with the opposite sex. (IS-9)

17. _____ Listening to the problems of others is boring; I become impatient. (IS-10)

Affect (iii)

18. _____ People cannot tell when I am happy, sad, or excited. (A-1)

19. _____ I rarely feel happy, sad, excited, or smile.

20. _____ I can easily tell when other people are happy, sad, or excited.

21. _____ I never worry about anything. (A-2)

22. _____ I never get angry or mad at people.

23. _____ I frequently experience feelings of anger and stress (A-3)

24. _____ I often hurt the feelings of my friends

25. _____ I often hit other people. (A-3, A-10)

26. _____ I often feel like I have a tremendous amount of energy (i.e., difficulty sleeping, constantly moving and talking). (A-4)

27. _____ I often feel like I have no energy and feel very sad. (A-5)

28. _____ I frequently feel depressed or "down in the dumps."

29. _____ I frequently feel like killing or hurting myself. (A-6)

30. _____ I often wish I were dead.

31. _____ I experience a lot of anxiety (A-7).

32. _____ I often experience excessive anxiety from one or more of the following: present or past problems with other people;

worry about the future (e.g., upcoming events); my life situation.

33. _____ I often experience excessive anxiety that frequently results in one or more of the following: inability to relax; muscle stiffness; sleep disturbance; worry; verbally talking about my problems to myself or others.

34. _____ It is easy for me to lose self control and exhibit too much laughing, crying, or anger. (A-8)

35. _____ I often become very, very scared along with one or more of the following: I get panicky; my heart beats fast; I experience shortness of breath. (A-9)

36. _____ Sometimes I get so mad I could kill people. (A-10)

37. _____ Sometimes I get so mad I hit people.

38. _____ I frequently get mad when others give me advice.

39. _____ People often tell me I have a bad temper.

Cognitive (iv)

40. _____ I do not like myself. (C-1)

41. _____ I frequently call myself names such as "stupid," "idiot," or "dumb."

42. _____ I usually fail when I try to do something.

43. _____ People like me.

44. _____ I do not trust people. (C-2)

45. _____ Other people frequently lie about me.

46. _____ My problems are overwhelming; they can't be solved. (C-3)

47. _____ I have no trouble solving problems involving other people.

48. _____ I have trouble forgetting familiar things I should remember, such as my address, my telephone number, and names of close friends or family. (C-4)

49. _____ I do not remember things as well as most people, such as names, what I did yesterday, or things in my past. (C-5)

50. _____ I don't have any problems. (C-7)

51. _____ I do not wish to make any changes in my life; I am happy the way things are. (C-6, C-7, C-8)

52. _____ When I have a problem I would rather leave it unsolved than to spend a lot of time trying to solve it. (C-9)

53. _____ I get mad if I spend too much time trying to solve a problem.

54. _____ I have difficulty following directions. (C-10).

55. _____ I do not like to follow directions given by other people.

Behavior (iii)

56. _____ It seems I always do what others want to do rather than what I would like to do. (B-1)

57. _____ During group discussion I find it hard to express my own views on a topic, especially when they differ from the views of other group members.

58. _____ I have difficulty concentrating on one thing for very long. (B-2)

59. _____ I never interrupt others during discussions. (B-3)

60. _____ I make people mad by saying or doing the wrong things.

61. _____ I find it difficult to look at the person to whom I am speaking. (B-4)

62. _____ People get mad at me when I tell them what I want. (B-5)

63. _____ I would rather others make decisions about major changes in my life. (B-6)

64. _____ When people do something I don't like I may not cooperate with them (e.g., put things off they want me to do; be stubborn; half heartedly participate in activities

with them; not do as good a job for them as I would otherwise). (B-6)

65. _____ I may yell at people and call them derogatory names (e.g., stupid; dumb) when they do something I don't like. (B-7)

66. _____ I frequently lose my temper and argue with people.

67. _____ I frequently lose my temper and hit people. (B-8)

Drugs (substance use or abuse, physical, and communication) (v)

68. _____ I frequently drink excessively at home or at a bar. (D-1.1)

69. _____ I take drugs during my leisure time.

70. _____ I do not have a substance abuse problem (D-1.2)

71. _____ I take drugs or drink alcohol to cope with my life stress and for relaxation. (D-1.3)

72. _____ I do not exercise regularly. (D-2.1)

73. _____ I bathe daily. (D-2.2)

74. _____ I frequently experience one or more of the following: insomnia, lack of muscular endurance, awkwardness. (D-2.3 through D-2.7)

75. _____ People have trouble understanding me when I speak. (D-3.1 through D-3.7)

Note for Examiner: Item numbers 4, 14, 16, 20, 43, 47, 59 and 73 should be scored by reversing the scale. These items are stated in the affirmative rather than in the negative. Item number 70 should be scored by reversing the scale if other assessments indicate the patient presently does not have a substance abuse problem.

PART III. POST INTERVIEW OBSERVATIONS

INSTRUCTIONS: Following termination of the above interview and dismissal of the examinee, the examiner should record the following post interview impressions using the scale below. Items requiring observation in music activities should be completed after observing the patient in music activities.

Very Inadequate 1	Inadequate 2	Mediocre 3	Adequate 4	Very Adequate 5

76. _____ Rate the examinee's eye contact.
77. _____ Rate the examinee's posture.
78. _____ Rate the examinee's grooming.
79. _____ Did the examinee appear motivated to engage in music therapy?
80. _____ Did the examinee exhibit appropriate facial expressions?
81. _____ Did the examinee engage in conversation, or what degree of conversational skill was observed?
82. _____ How was the examinee's concentration?
83. _____ How was the examinee's attention span?
84. _____ How was the examinee's retention (e.g., Did test questions have to be repeated?)?
85. _____ How well does the examinee use music (e.g., artistic; to reflect feelings or emotions; as an escape)?
86. _____ Rate the examinee's overall attitude toward music.
87. _____ Rate your initial impression of the quality of the examinee's overall interpersonal relationships.
88. _____ How does the examinee perceive or solve problems during music activities?
89. _____ Rate your initial impression of the examinee's overall level of self concept.
90. _____ Rate the examinee's abstracting ability (e.g., Did the examinee have trouble understanding the above questions?; did the examiner have to give a lot of examples?).

EXAMINER'S COMMENTS:

	Strongly Dislike	Dislike	Neutral	Like	Strongly Like
COUNTRY	1	2	3	4	5
POPULAR	1	2	3	4	5
ROCK	1	2	3	4	5
JAZZ	1	2	3	4	5
FOLK	1	2	3	4	5
RELIGIOUS	1	2	3	4	5
OTHER _____	1	2	3	4	5

Strongly Disagree 1	Disagree 2	Neutral 3	Agree 4	Strongly Agree 5

Appendix IV

Psychiatric Music Therapy Questionnaire: Adolescents

PATIENT IDENTIFICATION FORM

NAME _____ SEX _____ AGE _____

FORMAL/PRIMARY DIAGNOSIS:

AXIS I:_____

AXIS II:_____

AXIS III:_____

AXIS IV:_____

AXIS V: Current GAF: _____ Highest GAF past year: _____

TOTAL NUMBER AND LENGTH OF STAYS OF PRIOR HOSPITALIZATIONS:

HOSPITAL   LENGTH OF STAY

_____   _____

_____   _____

_____   _____

LENGTH OF HOSPITALIZATION AT PRESENT FACILITY _____

TYPES OF MEDICATION TAKEN *AND*   DOSAGE PRESCRIBED

_____   _____

_____   _____

PSYCHIATRIC MUSIC THERAPY QUESTIONNAIRE: ADOLESCENTS

INSTRUCTIONS: Parts I and II of the following questionnaire are to be administered by the <u>examiner, or therapist, interviewing the examinee, or patient</u>. Part III, Post Interview Observations, will be completed by the examiner following termination of the interview, or Part II.

EXAMINER: A major purpose of therapy is to assist you with problems that may be interfering with your ability to enjoy life to the fullest. The purpose of this questionnaire therefore, is to assist you in recognizing problems or "bad habits" you may have and wish to get rid of. Since these questions are personal, you may be assured of complete confidentiality. NO ONE WILL SEE YOUR ANSWERS OTHER THAN THE THERAPISTS. If you do not care to answer these questions simply tell me you do not care to answer these questions.

I. MUSIC (x)

1. EXAMINER: For the following styles of music tell me the number that indicates the degree you like each type of music (Examiner shows the following scale to the examinee).

	Strongly Dislike	Dislike	Neutral	Like	Strongly Like
COUNTRY	1	2	3	4	5
POPULAR	1	2	3	4	5
ROCK	1	2	3	4	5
JAZZ	1	2	3	4	5
FOLK	1	2	3	4	5
RELIGIOUS	1	2	3	4	5
OTHER _____	1	2	3	4	5

2. EXAMINER: Who is your favorite performer or composer?

(INSTRUCTION: Examiner writes in name below)

_____.

INSTRUCTIONS FOR EXAMINER: Give the examinee the scale, like the one below, attached to this questionnaire. The examinee may then refer to the scale as necessary when choosing a number.

EXAMINER: I am going to read some statements. After each statement tell me the number from this scale that describes the extent you agree with the statement.

Strongly Disagree	Disagree	Neutral	Agree	Strongly Agree
1	2	3	4	5

3. _____ I would like to learn to play a music instrument. (x)

4. _____ I would like to play a music instrument for others.

5. _____ I would probably enjoy playing a music instrument if I knew how (improvisation).

6. _____ I would like to participate in a group sing-a-long with a pianist or guitarist accompanying the group.

7. _____ I would like to learn to write music.

II. MULTIMODAL PROBLEM ANALYSIS

INSTRUCTIONS FOR EXAMINER: Let the examinee continue to keep the scale, like the one below. The examinee may then refer to the scale as necessary when choosing a number.

EXAMINER: I am going to read some statements. After each statement tell me the number from this scale that describes the extent you agree with the statement

Strongly Disagree	Disagree	Neutral	Agree	Strongly Agree
1	2	3	4	5

Affect (vi)

1. _____ Other people know when I am happy, sad, or excited. (A-1)
2. _____ I rarely feel happy, sad, or excited.
3. _____ I can easily tell when other people are happy, sad, or excited.
4. _____ I often hurt the feelings of my friends. (A-2)
5. _____ I often hit other people.
6. _____ I often get mad at others.
7. _____ I often get mad at myself.
8. _____ I often hurt or feel like hurting myself.
9. _____ I often feel like destroying things that others have.
10. _____ I don't fight with or yell at others.
11. _____ I often feel like I am under a lot of stress (A-3).
12. _____ Because of stress, I often experience one or more of the following: trouble sleeping, stomach aches, anxiety, and/or doing things I later regret.

13. _____ I experience a lot of anxiety (A-4).

14. _____ My excessive anxiety frequently results from one or more of the following: present or past problems with other people; worry about the future (e.g., upcoming events).

15. _____ I frequently do things I later am sorry for. (A-5)

16. _____ It is hard for me to tell other people about bad things that happen to me. (A-6)

17. _____ It is hard for me to tell other people about good things that happen to me.

18. _____ I frequently feel depressed or "down in the dumps." (A-7)

19. _____ I frequently feel like killing myself. (A-8)

20. _____ It is easy to say nice things to people. (A-9)

Interpersonal (vi)

21. _____ I rarely get into trouble for not following rules and regulations, or not doing what I am suppose to do. (IS-1)

22. _____ I have trouble following directions (e.g., Stay in your chair; Finish your work; Work quietly; Be nice to others).

23. _____ I like to take turns and to share my things with others.

24. _____ I frequently get into trouble on and off hospital/school grounds.

25. _____ I like to tell others when they make a mistake. (IS-2)

26. _____ I frequently call people names such as "stupid," "idiot," or "dumb."

27. _____ I would rather be alone than be with people. (IS-3)

28. _____ I find it hard to make friends.

29. _____ I have no close friends.

30. _____ It is hard for me to talk to people.

31. _____ It is hard for me to talk when in a group of people.

32. _____ I spend most of my leisure time with a gang or in a bar. (IS-4)

33. _____ I do not have a hobby; I rarely do something just for fun
        (IS-4 through IS-5)
34. _____ I would rather be alone or do nothing than to do
        something with other people. (IS-5 through IS-6)
35. _____ I have trouble listening to others when they talk to me.
        (IS-6)

Cognitive (vi)

36. _____ I do not like myself. (C-1)
37. _____ I frequently call myself names such as "stupid," "idiot," or "dumb."
38. _____ I usually fail when I try to do something.
39. _____ People do not like me.
40. _____ I have a lot of problems. (C-2)
41. _____ I have no trouble solving problems involving other people.
42. _____ When I have a problem I would rather leave it unsolved
        than to spend a lot of time trying to solve it. (C-3)
43. _____ I get mad if I spend too much time trying to solve a
        problem.
44. _____ I do not trust other people. (C-4)
45. _____ Other people frequently lie about me.
46. _____ It bothers me for someone to tell me how I could do
        something better. (C-5)
47. _____ I never have any problems. (C-6)
48. _____ I have trouble keeping track of things; I frequently lose
        things (e.g., bills, records, money). (C-7)
49. _____ I am always fighting with my parents. (C-8 through C-10)
50. _____ I have no trouble making decisions (e.g., What I would like
        to do each day; what to eat for dinner; where to go; what music
        to listen to; what clothes to wear). (C-13)

Drugs (substance use or abuse) (vii)

51. _____ Drugs will not hurt me psychologically or physically
       (D-1.1)
52. _____ I take drugs regularly. (D-1.1 through D-1.2)
53. _____ I do not have a substance abuse problem (D-1.2)
54. _____ I take drugs or drink alcohol to cope with my life stress,
       unpleasant situations, or to block unpleasant feelings.
       (D-1.2)

Behavior (vi)

55. _____ It seems I always do what others want to do rather than
       what I would like to do. (B-1)
56. _____ During group discussion I find it hard to express my own
       views on a topic, especially when they differ from the
       views of other group members.
57. _____ I have difficulty concentrating on, or doing one thing for
       very long. (B-2, B-5)
58. _____ I usually leave or keep to myself when in a group. (B-3)

Note for Examiner: Item numbers 1, 3, 10, 20, 21, 23, 41, and 50 should be
scored by reversing the scale. These items are stated in the affirmative
rather than in the negative. Item number 53 should be scored by reversing
the scale if other assessments indicate the patient presently does not have a
substance abuse problem.

PART III. POST INTERVIEW OBSERVATIONS

INSTRUCTIONS: Following termination of the above interview and dismissal of the examinee, the examiner should record the following post interview impressions using the scale below.

Very Inadequate 1	Inadequate 2	Mediocre 3	Adequate 4	Very Adequate 5

59. _____ Rate your initial impression of the quality of examinee's overall interpersonal relationships.

60. _____ How well does the examinee use music (e.g., artistic; to reflect feelings or emotions; as an escape)?

61. _____ How does the examinee perceive, perpetuate, or solve problems during music activities?

62. _____ How was the examinee's concentration?

63. _____ How was the examinee's attention span?

64. _____ How was the examinee's retention (e.g., Did test questions have to be repeated?)?

65. _____ Rate the examinee's eye contact.

66. _____ Rate the examinee's posture.

67. _____ Rate the examinee's grooming.

68. _____ Did the examinee appear motivated to engage in music therapy?

69. _____ Did the examinee exhibit appropriate facial expressions?

70. _____ Did the examinee engage in conversation, or what degree of conversational skill was observed?

71. _____ Rate your initial impression of the examinee's overall level of self concept.

72. _____ Rate the examinee's musical creativity or ability.

73. _____ Rate the examinee's overall attitude toward music.

EXAMINER'S COMMENTS:

	Strongly Dislike	Dislike	Neutral	Like	Strongly Like
COUNTRY	1	2	3	4	5
POPULAR	1	2	3	4	5
ROCK	1	2	3	4	5
JAZZ	1	2	3	4	5
FOLK	1	2	3	4	5
RELIGIOUS	1	2	3	4	5
OTHER _____	1	2	3	4	5

Strongly Disagree	Disagree	Neutral	Agree	Strongly Agree
1	2	3	4	5

Appendix V

Psychiatric Music Therapy Questionnaire: Childhood

PATIENT IDENTIFICATION FORM

NAME _____ SEX _____ AGE _____

FORMAL/PRIMARY DIAGNOSIS:

AXIS I:_____

AXIS II:_____

AXIS III:_____

AXIS IV:_____

AXIS V: Current GAF: _____ Highest GAF past year: _____

TOTAL NUMBER AND LENGTH OF STAYS OF PRIOR HOSPITALIZATIONS:

      HOSPITAL   LENGTH OF STAY

_____   _____

_____   _____

_____   _____

LENGTH OF HOSPITALIZATION AT PRESENT FACILITY _____

   TYPES OF MEDICATION TAKEN *AND*   DOSAGE PRESCRIBED

_____   _____

_____   _____

PSYCHIATRIC MUSIC THERAPY QUESTIONNAIRE
CHILDHOOD

INSTRUCTIONS FOR EXAMINER: Parts I and II of the following questionnaire are to be administered by the examiner, or therapist, <u>interviewing a second person (examinee) who is familiar with the child.</u> The examinee is to be dismissed after finishing Part II.

EXAMINER: A major purpose of therapy is to assist persons with problems that may be interfering with their ability to experience success in life. The purpose of this questionnaire therefore, is to assist you in recognizing your child's problems or inappropriate behavior that you would like to see changed. Since these questions are personal, you may be assured of complete confidentiality. NO ONE WILL SEE YOUR ANSWERS OTHER THAN THE THERAPISTS. If you do not care to answer these questions simply tell me you do not care to answer these questions.

I. MUSIC (xii)

1. INSTRUCTION: Examiner gives the attached music preference scale to the examinee.

EXAMINER: For the following styles of music tell me the number that indicates the degree <u>PATIENT'S NAME</u> likes each type of music. (xii)

	Strongly Dislike	Dislike	Neutral	Like	Strongly Like
COUNTRY	1	2	3	4	5
POPULAR	1	2	3	4	5
ROCK	1	2	3	4	5
JAZZ	1	2	3	4	5
FOLK	1	2	3	4	5
RELIGIOUS	1	2	3	4	5
OTHER _____	1	2	3	4	5

2. EXAMINER: Can you tell me <u>PATIENT'S NAME</u> favorite recording, performer, or composer? (INSTRUCTION: Examiner writes in name below)

_____.

INSTRUCTIONS FOR EXAMINER: Give the examinee the scale, like the one below, attached to this questionnaire. The examinee may then refer to the scale as necessary when choosing a number.

EXAMINER: I am going to read some statements. After each statement tell me the number from this scale that describes the extent the statement describes <u>PATIENT'S NAME</u>.

	Strongly Disagree 1	Disagree 2	Neutral 3	Agree 4	Strongly Agree 5

3. _____ Is able to identify characteristics of music such as style, slow or fast, which instruments are playing, and whether an instrument is playing or a person is singing. (xii)

4. _____ Sings melody in tune. (xii)

5. _____ Would enjoy playing a music instrument. (xii)

6. _____ Would enjoy making up own movements to music. (xii)

II. MULTIMODAL PROBLEM ANALYSIS

INSTRUCTIONS FOR EXAMINER: Let the examinee continue to keep the scale, like the one below. The examinee may then refer to the scale as necessary when choosing a number.

EXAMINER: I am going to read some statements. After each statement tell me the number from this scale that describes the extent the statement describes <u>PATIENT'S NAME.</u>

	Strongly Disagree 1	Disagree 2	Neutral 3	Agree 4	Strongly Agree 5

<u>Interpersonal</u> (vii)

1. _____ Rarely gets into trouble for not following rules and regulations, or not doing what he/she is suppose to do. (IS-1)

2. _____ Has trouble following directions (e.g., Stay in your chair; Finish your work; Work quietly; Be nice to others).

3. _____ Exhibits disruptive outbursts such as temper tantrums to attract attention.

4. _____ Is liked by peers.

5. _____ Frequently calls others names such as "stupid," "idiot," or "dumb."

6. _____ Does not talk, or talks very little with peers. (IS-2)

7. _____ Does not participate or avoids participating in group activities with peers.

8. _____ Is shy, timid, and not interested in peers.

9. _____ Argues with peers. (IS-3)

10. _____ Does not cooperate when working or playing with peers.

11. _____ Likes to take turns and to share things with others. (IS-4)

12. _____ Does not pay attention to others while participating in structured activities. (IS-5)

13. _____ Speaks too softly to be heard by others. (IS-6)

14. _____ Demonstrates good leadership skills (e.g., team captain). (IS-7)

15. _____ Does not express or respond to greetings or closings (e.g., good-byes; hellos). (IS-8)

Behavior (vii)

16. _____ Does not express needs or wants to others. (B-1)

17. _____ Goes along with the group instead of stating own opinions or feelings.

18. _____ Does not stay on task, is too easily distracted, and has poor concentration. (B-2)

19. _____ Grabs things from others instead of sharing or taking turns. (B-3)

20. _____ Hits peers. (B-4)

21. _____ Has poor eye contact; does not look at person speaking, or when speaking; looks away or down when speaking or being spoken to. (B-5)

Drugs (Motor) (viii)

22. _____ Awkward when attempting common movements such as walking. (D-1.1)
23. _____ Runs into people when in a group.
24. _____ Cannot use fingers to perform tasks as well as peers (e.g., picking up coins; grasping a pencil; dialing a telephone number; turning pages of a book [finger dexterity]). (D-1.2 through D-1.3)
25. _____ Catches ball, claps hands, hits toy drum with ease. (D-1.4)
26. _____ Often drops objects causing disruptions to others and embarrassment to self. (D-1.5)
27. _____ Cannot recall recent family events such as a trip to the park. (D-2.1)
28. _____ Has trouble imitating speech or sounds. (D-2.2)
29. _____ Talks too loud. (D-2.3)
30. _____ Does not pronounce words clearly. (D-2.4)
31. _____ Has trouble comprehending what is said to him or her. (D-2.5)

Cognitive (vii)

32. _____ Has trouble with following directions. (C-1)
33. _____ Understands concepts such as left and right, behind, in front of, and next to, or over, under, around, and through. (C-2)
34. _____ Makes negative comments about self, such as "I'm dumb," or "I'm not very smart." (C-3)
35. _____ Refuses to participate in group or individual activities because of a lack of self confidence (e.g., afraid of failure or ridicule). (C-3)

36. _____ Exhibits one or more of the following when performing tasks: disorganized rather than goal directed; fast without concern for quality rather than slow and deliberate; gives up easily rather than demonstrating perseverance; inaccurate rather than accurate. (C-4)

37. _____ Makes derogatory comments to peers if they don't do what he or she wants. (C-5)

38. _____ Has trouble telling what time it is, or the day of the week. (C-6)

39. _____ Has trouble counting money. (C-7)

40. _____ Has trouble memorizing the letters of the alphabet. (C-8)

41. _____ Has trouble counting. (C-9)

Affect (vii)

42. _____ Other people know when he or she is happy, sad, or excited. (A-1)

43. _____ Shows little or no emotion (e.g., happy, sad, or excited).

44. _____ Can easily tell when other people are happy, sad, or excited.

45. _____ Has trouble describing how others feel.

46. _____ Exhibits too many emotional extremes (e.g., laughing or crying; happy or sad).

47. _____ Emotions which are exhibited are frequently inappropriate for the occasion or situation (e.g., laughs in sad situations or when sad; cries when happy or in happy situations).

Note for Examiner: The above item numbers 1, 4, 11, 14, 25, 33, 42, and 44 should be scored by reversing the scale. These items are stated in the affirmative rather than in the negative.

PART III. POST INTERVIEW OBSERVATIONS

INSTRUCTIONS FOR THE EXAMINER: Part III, Post Interview Observations, is to be completed by the music therapist after observing the patient in music therapy. Rate items 48 through 62 using the following scale.

Very Inadequate 1	Inadequate 2	Mediocre 3	Adequate 4	Very Adequate 5

48. _____ Concentration
49. _____ Attention span
50. _____ Retention
51. _____ Interpersonal relationships
52. _____ Eye contact
53. _____ Posture
54. _____ Grooming
55. _____ Motivation to engage in music therapy
56. _____ Appropriate facial expressions
57. _____ Engages in conversation; degree of conversational skill
58. _____ Perceives and solves problems during music activities
59. _____ Uses music appropriately (e.g., artistic; to reflect feelings or emotions; as an escape)
60. _____ Musical creativity or ability
61. _____ Overall attitude toward music
62. _____ Rhythmic ability

63. Does the patient have any handicapping conditions that may impair activity participation?

YES   NO   (CIRCLE ONE)

(If YES, explain below under COMMENTS)

EXAMINER'S COMMENTS:

	Strongly Dislike	Dislike	Neutral	Like	Strongly Like
COUNTRY	1	2	3	4	5
POPULAR	1	2	3	4	5
ROCK	1	2	3	4	5
CHILDREN'S	1	2	3	4	5
FOLK	1	2	3	4	5
RELIGIOUS	1	2	3	4	5
OTHER _____	1	2	3	4	5

Strongly Disagree	Disagree	Neutral	Agree	Strongly Agree
1	2	3	4	5

Appendix VI

Clinical Forms

BASIC-ID

MODALITY   PROBLEMS

Behavior
_____
_____
_____
_____

Affect
_____
_____
_____
_____

Sensation
_____
_____
_____
_____

Imagery
_____
_____
_____
_____

Cognitive
_____
_____
_____
_____

Interpersonal
_____
_____
_____
_____

Drugs
_____
_____
_____
_____

Multimodal Music Therapy Profile: _____
(Adults)

I. MUSIC PREFERENCES

_____
_____
_____
_____
_____

II. MULTIMODAL PROBLEM ANALYSIS

Interpersonal	Problem	Music Therapy Intervention
____	_____	_____
____	_____	_____
____	_____	_____
____	_____	_____
____	_____	_____

Affect	Problem	Music Therapy Intervention
____	_____	_____
____	_____	_____
____	_____	_____
____	_____	_____

Cognitive	Problem	Music Therapy Intervention
____	_____	_____
____	_____	_____
____	_____	_____
____	_____	_____

Behavior	Problem	Music Therapy Intervention
____	_____	_____
____	_____	_____
____	_____	_____
____	_____	_____

Drugs	Problem	Music Therapy Intervention
____	_____	_____
____	_____	_____
____	_____	_____

III. POST INTERVIEW OBSERVATIONS

_____
_____
_____
_____

Multimodal Music Therapy Profile: _____
(Adolescents)

I. MUSIC PREFERENCES

_____
_____
_____
_____

II. MULTIMODAL PROBLEM ANALYSIS

Affect	Problem	Music Therapy Intervention
___	_____	_____
___	_____	_____
___	_____	_____
___	_____	_____

Interpersonal	Problem	Music Therapy Intervention
___	_____	_____
___	_____	_____
___	_____	_____
___	_____	_____

Cognitive	Problem	Music Therapy Intervention
___	_____	_____
___	_____	_____
___	_____	_____
___	_____	_____

Drugs	Problem	Music Therapy Intervention
___	_____	_____
___	_____	_____
___	_____	_____

Behavior	Problem	Music Therapy Intervention
___	_____	_____
___	_____	_____
___	_____	_____

III. POST INTERVIEW OBSERVATIONS

_____
_____
_____

Multimodal Music Therapy Profile: _____
(Childhood)

I. MUSIC PREFERENCES

_____
_____
_____

II. MULTIMODAL PROBLEM ANALYSIS

Interpersonal	Problem	Music Therapy Intervention
____	_____	_____
____	_____	_____
____	_____	_____
____	_____	_____

Behavior	Problem	Music Therapy Intervention
____	_____	_____
____	_____	_____
____	_____	_____
____	_____	_____

Drugs	Problem	Music Therapy Intervention
____	_____	_____
____	_____	_____
____	_____	_____

Cognitive	Problem	Music Therapy Intervention
____	_____	_____
____	_____	_____
____	_____	_____

Affect	Problem	Music Therapy Intervention
____	_____	_____
____	_____	_____
____	_____	_____

III. POST INTERVIEW OBSERVATIONS

_____
_____
_____

MUSIC THERAPY INTERVENTION PLAN

NAME: _____   CASE NO: _____

DATE OF ASSESSMENT _____

Music Therapy Goals and Objectives

* *

Goal #__ : _____
Goal Statement:_____

Objective #__ . __ : Objective Statement: _____
_____
_____
_____

Person Responsible: _____
Date Started: _____   Date Ended: _____
Reason Ended: _____

Objective #__ . __ : Objective Statement: _____
_____
_____
_____

Person Responsible: _____
Date Started: _____   Date Ended: _____
Reason Ended: _____

Objective #__ . __ : Objective Statement: _____
_____
_____
_____

Person Responsible: _____
Date Started: _____   Date Ended: _____
Reason Ended: _____
_____

IMPLEMENTATION STRATEGY

NAME: _____   CASE NO: _____

DATE OF ASSESSMENT _____

<u>OBJECTIVE #   . </u>
Materials Needed:_____

Reinforcement Schedule:_____

THERAPIST BEHAVIOR   PATIENT BEHAVIOR

_____   _____
_____   _____
_____   _____
_____   _____
_____   _____
_____   _____
_____   _____
_____   _____
_____   _____
_____   _____
_____   _____
_____   _____
_____   _____
_____   _____
_____   _____
_____   _____
_____   _____
_____   _____
_____   _____
_____   _____
_____   _____
_____   _____
_____   _____
_____   _____
_____   _____
_____   _____
_____   _____
_____   _____

Name of Agency _____

Music Therapy Progress Report Chart

Patient Name_____ Therapist Name _____

Specify goal and objective being worked on in the space provided. Place the appropriate evaluation code under the session date to indicate whether or not the objective was met, if the patient was absent, or if there was insufficient time to work on the objective. Write a session/monthly progress report.

Goal #____ :_____

_____ .

Objective #__ . __ : _____

_____

_____

Date: /   /   /   /   /   /
Progress:

EVALUATION:
Record a "+" for completion of objective.
Record a "-" for not meeting objective.
Record an "A" for patient or therapist being absent
Record an "0" for insufficient time during the session to work on the objective.

Session/Monthly Progress Report

REFERENCES

Adleman, E. J. (1985). Multimodal therapy and music therapy: Assessing and treating the whole person. *Music Therapy, 5,* 12–21.

American Psychiatric Association. (1987). *Diagnostic and statistical manual of mental disorders-revised (DSM-III-R).* Washington, D. C.: Author.

Bandler, R., & Grinder, J. (1975). *The structure of magic: A book about language and therapy* (Vol. 1). Palo Alto, California: Science and Behavior Books.

Britten, B. (1946). *The Young Person's Guide to the Orchestra.*

Cassity, M. D. (1977). Nontraditional guitar techniques for EMR and TMR residents in music therapy activities. *Journal of Music Therapy, 14,* 39–42.

Cassity, M. D. (1985). Techniques, procedures and practices employed in the assessment of adaptive and music behaviors of trainable mentally retarded children. *Dissertation Abstracts International, 46,* 10A. (Ann Arbor: University Microfilms International No. 85-27959, 2955.)

Cassity, M. D. & Cassity, J. E. (1994). Psychiatric music therapy assessment and treatment in clinical training facilities. *Journal of Music Therapy, 31,* 2–30.

Cassity, M. D. & Theobold, K. A. (1990). Domestic violence: Assessments and treatments employed by music therapists. *Journal of Music Therapy, 27,* 179–194.

Egan, G. (1990). *The skilled helper: A systematic approach to effective helping.* Belmont, California: Brooks/Cole Publishing Company.

Lazarus, A. A. (1976). *Multimodal behavior therapy.* New York: Springer.

Lazarus, A. A. (1989). *The practice of multimodal therapy.* Baltimore: The John Hopkins University Press.

Lloyd, N. (1968). *The golden encyclopedia of music.* New York: Golden Press.

Rubin, B. (1976). Handbells in therapy. *Journal of Music Therapy, 13,* 49–53.

Spitzer, R. L., Gibbon, M., Skodol, A. E., Williams, J. B. W., and First, M. B. (1989). *DSM-III-R case book.* Washington, D. C.: American Psychiatric Press, Inc., pp. 90–93.